BEYOND YOUR BACKYARD

BEYOND YOUR BACKYARD

STEPPING OUT TO SERVE OTHERS

TOM ELLSWORTH

Standard®
PUBLISHING
Bringing The Word to Life

Cincinnati, Ohio

Published by Standard Publishing, Cincinnati, Ohio
www.standardpub.com

Copyright © 2008 Standard Publishing

Project editor: Lynn Lusby Pratt
Cover and interior design: The Tenfold Collective

ISBN 978-0-7847-2108-7

Library of Congress Cataloging-in-Publication Data
Ellsworth, Tom, 1955-
      Beyond your backyard : stepping out to serve others / Tom Ellsworth.
         p. cm.
      Includes bibliographical references and index.
      ISBN 978-0-7847-2108-7 (perfect bound : alk. paper)
      1. Evangelistic work. 2. Service (Theology) I. Title.
      BV3770.E45 2008
      269'.2--dc22

                  2007035190

14 13 12 11 10 09 08 9 8 7 6 5 4 3 2 1

For my parents, Tom and Midge Ellsworth,
and
my wife's parents, Floyd and Alma Barrow.
Thank you for giving us, your children,
wonderful homes and great backyards
in which to grow.
More importantly, thank you for showing us
how to get beyond our backyards
to love and serve God!

I never cease to be amazed at God's grace. He not only provides for our needs as promised, but sometimes he gives us our dreams on a silver platter. As I worked on this book, I realized he had made another of my dreams a reality. But isn't that just like God? He is a Father who loves to give good gifts to his children—and he has given me more than my fair share:

My wife, Elsie. For over thirty years she has been the best gift of my life. That she chose to share her life's journey with me still makes me feel like I'm living a dream. I am deeply grateful for her encouragement, wisdom, and love. Without her help and patience, I never could have undertaken such a project.

My daughters, Emily and Rebekah. Not even in my dreams could I have envisioned two young women who would enrich my life so incredibly. Being their dad continues to be the greatest adventure of my life.

My spiritual family at Sherwood Oaks Christian Church. For the last twenty-seven years, I have been privileged to serve and worship with this wonderful congregation. I am indebted to the leadership, staff, and congregation for their gracious support.

My editors, Dale Reeves and Lynn Pratt, at Standard Publishing. Their encouraging words kept me going, and their editorial skills kept me focused. I am grateful!

My friend Mark Atteberry. As an author, Mark inspired me to dream about being a writer. As a friend, he encouraged me to *become* one.

And you! Thank you for taking time to read this book. I hope and pray that it will encourage you to get out of your own backyard and change the world for Jesus Christ!

INTRODUCTION   9

1   STUCK IN THE MUD   14
1 SAMUEL 13:13, 14

2   PLAY NICE!   29
EXODUS 2:1-10; 18:1-8; NUMBERS 12:1, 2

3   ROOF-CRASHIN' FRIENDS   45
MARK 2:1-12; LUKE 5:17-26

4   DOIN' GOOD IN THE HOOD   60
LUKE 10:25-37

5   OUT ON A LIMB   75
LUKE 19:1-10

6   BACKYARD BULLIES   90
LUKE 22:47-51; JOHN 18:1-11

7   BEYOND THE HEDGE   107
ACTS 17:16-34

8   IN THE NAME OF JESUS   124
ACTS 3:1-19

NOTES   140

The highest form of worship is the worship of unselfish Christian service. The greatest form of praise is the sound of consecrated feet seeking out the lost and helpless.
BILLY GRAHAM

I learned it years ago, and I suspect you did too:

Here's the church,
(fold hands with fingers hidden inside)

here's the steeple;
(point both index fingers up, forming a spire)

open the doors
(open thumbs)

and see all the people.
(turn hands over and wiggle fingers)

It was an entertaining exercise for me as a small child. Unfortunately, it was all too descriptive of the local church in many places. I'm not sure why it happens, but at times the church becomes content with being willfully sequestered inside the walls of its buildings. In those cases, to learn about the church, you have to go where the church meets. To see the church in action, you have to attend a church service. To discover the truth about Jesus Christ, you have to seek out the answers from inside the church building.

Jesus talks about Christians being salt and light in the *world* (Matthew 5:13-16). Where did we get the idea that the salt needs to be locked up behind doors? When did we decide that the light needs to be filtered through stained glass? One of my college professors observed that there were only two buildings where a person could not see what was going on inside: a tavern and a church. One usually had darkened windows and the other, stained glass. It was a bit of an exaggeration at the time, but not much. From the outside of the church it was impossible to know what was happening inside. One had to "open the doors and see all the people."

Long before Las Vegas began its newest advertising blitz, some congregations and some individual Christians were practicing a similar philosophy: "What happens in the church stays in the church." It hasn't always been like that, you know. In the first century, the church was not defined by its four walls. It was not confined to a worship service or to a predictable weekly pattern.

Don't get me wrong. I love the church! I am thankful for the church building and property that enhances kingdom ministry. Several years ago we experienced a church fire and spent two years in a high school auditorium. I know how valuable a good building can be! I'm also thankful for the excitement and inspiration that result from worshiping with others who share a common faith and worldview. Some of the most life-changing moments I've ever experienced have come during worship with other Christians. And let's face it, the first-century church wasn't perfect or problem free—I'm not sure I would have wanted to minister in Corinth!

Here's the problem: it is all too easy to become inward focused instead of outward focused, if we aren't careful. Our first-century counterparts may have struggled with that issue as much as we do. Oh sure, we are still passionate for the truth, we still desire to exalt Jesus Christ, and we still long for the moment of his return. But in some ways we've lost the urgency of the *go*! It is so easy to become satisfied to offer the invitation to *come*. Anyone who makes it past the front doors is welcome.

In the future, I don't believe *come* will have much of an impact. Tomorrow's generations of unbelievers will not be drawn to the church behind four walls, but to the church that is found serving in local food pantries, homeless shelters, and hospices. We cannot do less than *go!* Christians of all generations are called to demonstrate their love, share their faith, and serve humanity . . . all for the privilege of introducing others to Jesus.

For the last several years, my good friend Steve Connor has served with Sports Outreach International.[1] In his global work, Steve holds to this philosophy: "If they play in your backyard, and if they play in your front yard, then maybe someday they'll come play in your house." I like that. It's a concept worth embracing. But before we can expect others to come and play in our yard, we must meet them on their turf. Many people may not be interested in coming to a building . . . for a variety of reasons:

o   *a bad experience with a church in the past*

o   *a negative perception of what happens in a church building*

o   *the counterproductive influence of hypocrites*

o   *the fear of entering a place where they will be the outsiders*

Seekers who might resist coming to a building would still love to meet Jesus. So let's take a step out of our comfort zones and meet them where they are.

I know. It can be a bit unnerving to move beyond the safety of the church doors. But in the ancient church, Christians permeated the world around them; they became salt and light. Our predecessors left behind a great legacy for us to follow. Study the mini biographies of first-generation disciples like Tabitha, Barnabas, Lydia, Titus, Epaphroditus, and Aquila and Priscilla. They changed their world because they went into the world to reach others. We too can add our light and flavor to the world. As a matter of fact, many Christians are doing exactly that. You'll read about a few of them in this book.

I still believe the two-fisted children's poem has value. But as we look to the future, I would suggest we teach a slightly modified poem to our kids:

> Here's the church,
>
> here's the steeple;
>
> open the doors
>
> and *send out* the people!

Now is the time to break out of our four walls. Knock down the doors and send out the people. There is no limit to the number of practical ways in which you can serve others in the name of Jesus—and make an eternal difference. The adventure is yours for the taking. Go! Get beyond your backyard!

When one door closes, another opens; but we often look so long and so regretfully upon the closed door that we do not see the one which has opened for us.
ALEXANDER GRAHAM BELL

Does the name Elisha Gray ring a bell? It would if Alexander Graham Bell hadn't won the race to the U.S. Patent Office.

On February 14, 1876, both men applied for a patent for what would later become the telephone.[1] On Gray's application he described his apparatus "for transmitting vocal sounds telegraphically." Unfortunately, Elisha Gray was two hours too slow. After years of litigation, Bell was legally named the inventor of the telephone.

What makes the story more painful is the fact that Gray had a better invention. It was later discovered that the apparatus described in Gray's application would have worked, while that in Bell's patent would not have. Think about it—Gray missed the opportunity of a lifetime by only two hours.

Elisha Gray isn't the only member of the Missed Opportunity Club. Consider these other regretful decisions:

o *Texas businessman Ross Perot had the opportunity to buy Microsoft in 1979 and turned it down. He didn't think it was worth the price.[2]*

o *In 1938 Joe Schuster and Jerry Siegel, the two teenagers who conceived the idea of the Man of Steel, sold Superman to DC Comics for less than two hundred dollars.[3]*

o *In the 1984 NBA draft, the Houston Rockets and the Portland Trail Blazers both passed over a very qualified, young jump shooter, making Michael Jordan the third draft pick of that season.*[4]

o *Today it costs around $705,000 for a thirty-second commercial on American Idol,*[5] *the number one show in the U.S. But back in 2002 when the show's creators were looking for a market here in America, none of the major networks were interested. Only Fox network expressed an interest—and since then they've been laughing all the way to the bank.*

You might expect God's Word to contain only success stories. Indeed there are plenty of biographical narratives of successful Bible characters, men and women who saw an opportunity and made a true difference in the lives of others:

o *We are emboldened when reading about how Moses—who stood face-to-face against Pharaoh, the most powerful ruler of his day—rescued the enslaved Hebrew nation (Exodus 7–12).*

o *We are inspired when reading about a widow who put everything she had in the offering, trusting God to supply all her future financial needs (Mark 12:41-44).*

o *We are challenged when reading about a young boy who willingly gave up his lunch, which Jesus took and used to feed five thousand hungry men, plus women and children (Matthew 14:13-21).*

But not every narrative ends so triumphantly. Some Bible biographies recount the lives of those who let opportunity slip through their fingers. Instead of seizing the moment, they got stuck in the mud. Immobilized. Powerless. Helpless. Incapable. They never lived up to their God-given potential. Just think of the squandered lives we read about in Scripture.

The Bible mentions several of the charter members of the Missed Opportunity Club:

o *Samson was physically strong but morally weak. He could have been an inspirational leader, but his character got stuck in the mud of immorality. Instead of leaving behind a great legacy, he let his God-given gifts languish in a dusty, Philistine gristmill (Judges 13–16).*

o *Nicodemus was an influential member of the Jewish Sanhedrin and a respected leader among his peers. He could have stood up as a powerful advocate for Jesus, but his faith got stuck in the mud of his fears. Instead of serving Christ boldly, he hovered around in the dark shadows of wannabe discipleship (John 3).*

o *Ananias and Sapphira were semi-affluent members of the Jerusalem church, who were momentarily celebrated for their generous giving. Their contribution should have been a wonderful example to the early church, but they got stuck in the mud of their greed. They gave only part of the sale price of their land to the church—and there was nothing wrong with that—but they insisted that it was the total price. Such bold-faced deceit cost them much more than they ever intended to pay. Instead of dropping a gift into the offering plate, they dropped dead at the feet of the ushers! (Acts 5).*

o *Eli was a faithful high priest but a lousy father. Eli's two sons, Hophni and Phinehas, were an embarrassment to God—and should have been to Eli. They had the opportunity to follow in their father's footsteps, but they got stuck in the mud of their pride and hypocrisy. They went into battle arrogantly leading the ark of the covenant; but they did not survive, and the ark did not come home. Eli, instead of enjoying his golden years, collapsed at the news and died of a broken neck—and more importantly, a broken heart (1 Samuel 2–4).*

o *Demas was an associate of the apostle Paul, but he was known as a quitter. Demas had the opportunity to assist the imprisoned Paul with the greatest mission in the world, but he got stuck in the mud of envy. Instead of loving God with all his heart, he chose to love the world with all his desire (2 Timothy 4:10).*

OPPORTUNITY KNOCKS

Can you relate to any of those people? Have you ever missed an opportunity to make a difference? Do you ever find your faith stuck in the mud?

We could learn from the lives of many different characters, but we'll focus on just one in this chapter. He had great potential for God and tremendous opportunities to make a difference; but he got mired down in the mud of his own self-importance, and he never came clean. (Had Saul lived up to his potential, it is possible we never would have heard of a shepherd boy named David.) We meet this mediocre monarch in the book of 1 Samuel.

Saul's story begins with stubborn people and missing donkeys—which, by the way, are very similar! In the days of the judges, the Israelites reached the conclusion that they wanted to be like every other country. After all, they were the only nation without a king. In truth, they *had* a king. The Israelites had long lived in a theocratic system of government—God was their ruler and sovereign. But since he wasn't present in flesh and blood, the Israelites felt slighted. Obviously, they sacrificed all common sense when they made this appeal for a king. What were they thinking? *We want to trade the impartial, benevolent, providential grace of God for a fickle, subjective, self-exalted ruler who will draft our young men into military service and will tax our wages to provide for his extravagant palace and lavish lifestyle.* It was a lousy trade, but then . . . peer pressure is hard to resist.

When we think about dealing with peer pressure, teenagers usually come to mind. But adults are certainly not immune. When an individual believes he is missing something valuable or enjoyable because everyone else has it or is doing it, that's peer pressure. Such pressure is a powerful force unless strong convictions prevail.

My *preferences* are easily manipulated by peer pressure. I might prefer to eat at a particular restaurant, but if the other three people in the car want to eat elsewhere, I will concede. A *conviction*, however, is not subject to peer pressure; it is a core belief that will not be compromised at any cost. For example, a conviction regarding the truth of Christ's resurrection is what led to the martyrdom of the apostles. A conviction that the world needed to know the gospel compelled Paul to endure every possible pain and discomfort to fulfill that mission.

A conviction is not just something that you hold; it is something that holds *you*. A conviction will control your ways, your words, and your wealth. It is vital to determine whether faith is a preference or a conviction. The crowd is easy to follow but, all too often, painfully wrong.

A few years ago a snowstorm hit Bloomington less than forty-eight hours before the weekly trash pickup day. I anticipated that the pickup would be delayed due to the harsh weather, but I couldn't confirm that hunch. I checked in the newspaper and online. The Department of Sanitation was no help since it was closed. My only recourse was to watch the neighbors. Without exception, everyone on our street set out their trash that night for the early morning pickup, so I decided to follow suit. I reasoned that the whole street couldn't possibly be wrong. But we *were*. Pickup was delayed until later in the week.

I realize, of course, that being confused about our weekly garbage is a trivial matter. Still, it was a cold reminder that when I decided to follow the crowd, I was left holding the bag—the trash bag. Don't get stuck in the mud of peer pressure, or you too will end up with nothing but garbage.

Peer pressure notwithstanding, the Almighty decided to give the obstinate Israelites what they kept insisting they wanted: a king. Now remember, there is more to the story than stubborn people—there is also a herd of missing donkeys. An influential Benjamite named Kish had a son named Saul, who is described as impressive, without equal among the Israelites, and a head taller than any others (1 Samuel 9:1, 2). He definitely would have been the number one NBA draft choice! One day Kish's herd of donkeys went AWOL, so Saul and a servant were given the task of locating the wayward animals.

Saul was completely unaware that God had chosen him to be king, but the Lord revealed it to Samuel, the last of the spiritual judges to lead Israel. Look closely at this story, and you will see the providential work of God at every turn. It seemed to Saul that the donkeys had vanished without a trace. For three days Saul and the servant carefully searched the area, but neither of them could find a clue as to the herd's whereabouts. The servant suggested they seek an answer from a "man of God; he is highly respected, and everything he says comes true" (v. 6). Isn't it interesting that Saul didn't think of that first? It would seem that the spiritual element wasn't a priority with him.

As they entered the town, the man of God, Samuel, met them on his way to the place of sacrifice. Perfect timing. However, Saul didn't even know Samuel. He approached Samuel and asked for the location of the prophet's home. Amazing! Had he never attended a sacrifice presided over by Samuel? Had he never heard the prophet speak on behalf of God? How does one grow up just down the road from the greatest spiritual leader of his time and not know him?

Before Saul could pose the question of the day, Samuel explained, "The donkeys you lost three days ago . . . have been found" (v. 20). He then informed Saul that he was to be the guest of honor at the feast. He got the best cut of meat, sat at the head of the table, and spent the night in the prophet's home. The next morning as he prepared to return home, Saul got the shock of a lifetime. Samuel took a jar of oil and poured it on Saul's head, stating that the Lord was anointing him as the new king (10:1). Then Samuel told Saul that on his way home he would meet two men who would tell him about the donkeys, then three men would offer him two loaves of bread, and finally he would join a band of prophets and prophesy with them (vv. 2-6).

Disappearing donkeys, being the guest of honor at the feast (and the only one with filet mignon), meeting total strangers who offered him free bread, and singing baritone with the Prophets of Praise ensemble were not coincidental experiences. God was very much at work.

News-breaking miracles are not a daily occurrence, but the providential work of God *is*. Every day God works in our lives to accomplish his will. God is at work in your life whether you can see it or not. Even when you feel like your life is stuck in the mud, God may be doing his greatest work in you! Do not lose heart.

A HUMBLE BEGINNING

When the day came for Saul to be officially anointed as king over Israel, he was so afraid and humble that he hid. He did not come out from hiding until he was found and forced to appear. It was an exciting day— the people were ecstatic. They had their king, and he was impressive! But in the midst of all of the wonderful celebration came this footnote to the day: "Some troublemakers said, 'How can this fellow save us?' They despised him and brought him no gifts" (10:27).

No celebration is without its naysayers, pessimists, and whiners. Some people are never satisfied. Earlier, they didn't like it because they had no king; then they didn't like the king God had chosen. I can hear them whispering behind their hands: *Just because he's tall, dark, and handsome he gets to be king. If he thinks I'm going to give him a new toaster for his palace-warming, he can think again.* But Saul kept silent.

Saul had so much going for him. He was handpicked, blessed, and transformed by God. At thirty years of age, he had the presence of a celebrity and the look of royalty, but he was a man of humility. When he could have retaliated at such rude and brazen behavior, he just kept silent and went about his business. I like that. And his next move was even more endearing. He didn't start building his palace, creating a tax structure, or assembling an army; he humbly went back home to the farm.

His first big test challenged his military leadership. An Ammonite king was terrorizing the Jewish city of Jabesh. The rogue offered a treaty that would have called for every person in the city to lose his right eye. Not much of a treaty, is it? When word reached Saul, the Spirit of the Lord came upon him; and he took action. Saul rallied the troops and attacked the Ammonite army at night in their own camp, destroying them (11:1-11). That day he gained the confidence and loyalty of the people. Everything was looking great. Saul demonstrated noble qualities that are worth emulating: a humble attitude, a simple manner, a magnanimous heart, and a courageous spirit.

HUMBLE PIE

No wonder God chose Saul. He had such potential . . . until he got caught up in himself. Saul appears to be a man driven by the external. Perhaps he started believing his own press—what others said about him—or simply concluded that he could do anything since he was king.

Regardless, he lost his humility and made a grave error in judgment on the eve of a later battle.

When he saw his army beginning to scatter because of fear of the Philistines, he no longer waited for Samuel to come and offer the sacrifice before God. Saul offered the sacrifice himself. This was no act of worship; it was merely a perfunctory ritual before battle. It was not carried out in faith, but in fear. This offering was not about God; it was about a good-luck charm. It was not in Saul's job description to offer the sacrifice of worship. And the spirit in which he made the sacrifice was unacceptable. Just because he was God's chosen man for the throne didn't give him the right to ignore God's command.

Saul was still wiping the blood off his hands when Samuel appeared and gave him this tragic indictment: "'You acted foolishly,' Samuel said. 'You have not kept the command the LORD your God gave you; if you had, he would have established your kingdom over Israel for all time. But now your kingdom will not endure; the LORD has sought out a man after his own heart and appointed him leader of his people, because you have not kept the LORD's command'" (13:13, 14).

It would be some time before David entered the picture, but God began at that point to move in a new direction. Saul became indecisive, melancholy, defensive, and inactive. He no longer knew which way to turn. Should he fight or retreat? Should he lead or retire? He just wallowed in the mud of uncertainty. And so it seems that Saul began to respond only to outward circumstances rather than being driven by the inward leading of God's Spirit.

First Samuel 15 records the next assignment Saul received from God. He was to destroy the Amalekites who waylaid and attacked the Israelites as they came up from Egypt. God instructed him to destroy everything and everyone—not even the livestock were to be spared. Once again Saul stepped in the mud of disobedience. He spared Agag the king, and Saul's men saved the best of the herds for themselves. Following the battle Saul erected a monument in his own honor, and he went to Carmel to prepare a celebration feast where he planned to parade the captured king as his trophy of battle. God, in his anger, sent Samuel with tragic news on a day of triumph. When Samuel arrived, Saul blurted out, "I have carried out the LORD's instructions" (15:13).

That was a whopper. So Samuel asked, "Why then do I hear sheep and cows?"

"Because the men saved back the best to sacrifice to God," Saul responded. Another whopper. They had done nothing of the sort; they fully intended to keep the best of the flocks and herds for themselves. When we get caught with a hand in the cookie jar, we often try to put a spiritual spin on our unspiritual deeds.

Samuel then spoke words worth remembering: "What is more pleasing to the LORD: your burnt offerings and sacrifices or your obedience to his voice? Obedience is far better than sacrifice" (v. 22, *NLT*). Finally Saul admitted, "I was afraid of the people and so I gave in to them" (v. 24). From that day forward God rejected Saul as king and was sorry he had ever placed Saul in that royal role. Saul continued on until the time for David to take the throne, reigning for forty-two years—but most of those years were without God's blessing.

Saul was a hero among his people even though he had been rejected by God. He had achieved great military victories, established Israel as a powerful nation, and made the land prosperous. The average citizen of Israel sang his praises, but praises of the people are not the praises that matter. With the passing of time, Saul became a bitter, angry, vengeful man. On numerous occasions, even though he knew God had rejected him and his sons as the royal line, Saul tried to kill David to prevent him from becoming the next king. In the end Saul became so desperate and stooped so low that he consulted a witch for spiritual answers. And she rebuked him for it! (1 Samuel 28). His finish is one of the saddest in Scripture. He had so much to offer but offered so little. His life is a testimony on how *not* to be a servant.

One of the convincing evidences for the inspiration of Scripture is the fact that it includes these human failures as well as the successes—and there *are* more tragedies than triumphs. We can learn relevant lessons from the examples (sometimes poor ones) of people who lived during Bible times. Consider the following imperatives from Saul's life.

HUMBLE YOURSELF

Humble yourself before the Lord, or you will get stuck in the mud of self-absorption. Saul began his reign humbly but soon let his pride push humility into the shadow of his character. Humility remains one of the most endearing traits of true leadership. Jim Collins, writing in *Good to Great*, explored the characteristics of leaders who turned good companies into great companies. He identified the best as level-five leaders. One would expect such leaders to be arrogant in their own success. Just the opposite was true—humility was a characteristic they all had in common.[6]

We are never more like Jesus than when we live unassuming lives. Of all God's creation, only human beings are capable of willful arrogance. Yet what do we have to be arrogant about? Regardless of who you are, what you do, or how much you know, no one has any bragging rights. Each of us has sinned; that's the common denominator of the human race. And each of us is dependent upon God's grace; that's our common hope. If the

Creator himself was known as the humblest of men when he lived in this world, who are we to aim for anything less?

Saul could have been the best of kings, but his reign ended tragically because somewhere along the way he strayed from the path of humility and stepped into the mud of his own selfish agenda.

OBEY THE LORD

Only God's opinion matters, and he considers obedience more important than any sacrifice of worship. Peter Bulkeley wrote, "If God be God over us we must yield him universal obedience in all things. He must not be over us in one thing, and under us in another, but he must be over us in every thing."[7]

God's instructions are not to be considered as suggestions. Live long enough in this world, and you will learn that God's principles are for your benefit. Therefore, obey God. Follow him, even if the world celebrates you as a hero. Follow him, even if you like your direction better. Follow him, even if everything in you rebels against his lead. Obey him, and you will guard against becoming self-deceived.

HONOR THE LORD

When Saul should have been giving credit to God, he was building monuments to himself. Isn't it interesting that we don't have any record of Saul praying? He had prophesied at times, but for divine guidance he relied upon other prophets, dreams, or the high priest's Urim and Thummim (see 1 Samuel 28:6; Exodus 28:30).

At times he showed remorse, but only God knows whether or not he was truly repentant. There seems to be little, if any, personal relationship with the Lord. This much is true: Saul's royal reign did not honor God. Ironic, isn't it? The one who elevated Saul from being a plowboy to king got lost in the shuffle of power. Does that ever happen in your life? The one who supplied you with talents and abilities gets overlooked while you get the praise as you exercise those talents and abilities. How easily we forget God's benefits. The Lord alone deserves the honor and the credit for any good we may do.

Saul got stuck in the mud of this world and never got out of its muck and mire. A life that was so full of potential ended tragically empty.

There is a clue at the beginning of the story that explains why Saul did not finish well: he didn't know the man of God just down the road. I can't help but wonder whether God had ever truly been an active part of Saul's life. No throne, golden crown, or princely title can compensate for not knowing the King of kings and what he's doing.

Take a peek over the fence. God is working in the lives of people, but we may not notice if we are stuck in the mud of our own backyards. To finish well in this life, spend time serving others in the Lord's name. Don't miss the opportunities God sends your way.

I love to hear the service stories of Christ-followers. Like so many other churches, our congregation is making a concerted effort to impact our community with sincere acts of service. Our missions ministry hosts an annual autumn CareFest. With this event church families blanket the area by trying to meet the needs of various community groups or organizations. They have worked with the local school corporation, Boys Club/Girls Club, humanitarian groups, the city's parks and recreation department, and more. In a day's time, a thousand volunteers can make a big dent in the mound of unmet needs. In most cases the church furnishes both the labor and the supplies for the work. It is a great way to bridge gaps and share the compassion of Christ. I've watched families have a great time serving together. From the oldest to the youngest, they work with a sense of satisfaction seldom seen in other chores. As people work together they also talk, laugh, and grow together.

It is amazing how serving Christ improves one's whole outlook on life. And the best part is, *any* congregation can reach this goal! Size or location is immaterial. Look for the unmet needs of your community, offer to help out, and then *go*—clean, rake, paint, build, plant . . . Your congregation can do it; *you* can do it!

King Saul could have made an incredible difference as Israel's first monarch, but he let divine opportunities slip through his fingers and fall into the mud of the palace backyard. The same thing can happen to each of us if we aren't careful.

You are gifted by God. Don't hide from God's leading like Saul did. Don't allow yourself to get wrapped up in your own self-promotion like Saul did. Don't get stuck in the mud of this world like Saul did. Stay focused on the Lord, and follow him wherever he leads!

1 Some Bible biographies recount the lives of those who let opportunity slip through their fingers. Instead of seizing the moment, they got stuck in the mud. Immobilized. Powerless. Helpless. Incapable.

Have you ever felt that way? What opportunities do you wish you had back? What can you do to guarantee that future opportunities won't slip away?

2 Saul demonstrated noble qualities that are worth emulating: a humble attitude, a simple manner, a magnanimous heart, and a courageous spirit.

Why do those character traits transcend time and culture? Take an honest inventory of your life. Are those traits obvious in your daily living? If not, what do you need to do in order to ensure that they will become a part of your character?

3 When Saul should have been giving credit to God, he was building monuments to himself.

Why are we so reluctant to give God the credit for the positive things that happen in our lives? Are we afraid that if we honor God it will somehow take away from our accomplishments? What can you do to change your attitude about giving credit where credit is due?

4 [Saul's] finish is one of the saddest in Scripture. He had so much to offer but offered so little.

What other Bible leaders fell short of their potential? What caused their downfall? If you desire to finish well, what specific action steps will you need to take to accomplish that goal?

Our children are the living messages we send into a time we shall not see.
ART LINKLETTER

Tom and Alleta Sullivan had five sons and one daughter in the span of eight years.[1] They were living life like most other middle-class families in Waterloo, Iowa—until the outbreak of World War II. That's when they received the news that Bill Ball, a family friend, had died on the USS *Arizona* in the attack on Pearl Harbor. The next month, January 1942, all five Sullivan brothers enlisted in the Navy, with one stipulation—they wanted to serve together. The Navy granted their request. By November of that year, George, Frank, Joe, Madison, and Albert Sullivan were fighting in the battle of Guadalcanal aboard the light cruiser USS *Juneau*. Unfortunately, in the fury of the battle, the cruiser was torpedoed twice and sank. All five of the Sullivans perished in the Pacific. Only ten crewmen of the USS *Juneau* were rescued, but the survivors had no difficulty remembering the Sullivan boys' motto: "We stick together!"

That's what families do. They stick together—in good times and bad, in the fun moments as well as the sad. And each member of the family fills an indispensable role.

If you grew up with siblings, you most likely spent time playing in the backyard. How many times did one of your parents holler out the back door, "You kids play nice!"? Siblings have a reputation for fighting like cats and dogs when they are alone, but let some outside force try to break into the backyard . . . and the family members unite to defend one another against all odds.

If you have a brother or sister, you have been both elated and exasperated that you do. If you don't have siblings, you have been both elated and exasperated that you don't. Having siblings not only teaches us valuable lessons about life in general but, more importantly, also provides insight into being a part of God's family. Bible history records some unique sibling stories: Cain and Abel, Jacob and Esau, Peter and Andrew, James and John . . . and of course, the twelve sons of Israel.

There is one sibling relationship, however, that is frequently overlooked. In the adventure of the exodus from Egypt, Moses is usually studied as the prince of Egypt or the great deliverer of Israel, but not very often as the brother of Miriam. From their journey together, we can learn a lot about serving our families and serving within the family of God.

DON'T WORRY; I'VE GOT YOUR BACK

I'm not sure how it would have been phrased in Moses' day 3,500 years ago, but "Don't worry; I've got your back" is an encouraging statement I would always welcome from a sibling—or for that matter, from any other member of the family.

Amram and Jochebed were expecting a child at the worst possible time. The slavery they had endured in Egypt was bad enough, but now the slightly paranoid Pharaoh feared the Hebrew slaves were growing into a huge nation that could rebel against his rule. Consequently, Pharaoh issued a decree to the Hebrew midwives that every male child born to a slave couple was to be put to death at the moment of birth. Because the midwives feared God more than they feared Pharaoh, they refused to carry out the death sentence. They let the boys live. It didn't take Pharaoh long to figure out that his plan was not working, so he issued a second decree instructing that all Hebrew male babies be thrown into the Nile River.

Have you ever tried to keep a baby quiet? Only God knows how many Hebrew boys were discovered and tossed into the Nile.

The Nile is home to the largest species of crocodiles in Africa, so the sorrow of losing an infant son was only punctuated by the cruelty of how he died. The blood of slave children mingled with the waters of the mighty river. Eighty years later when Moses returned to free the Hebrew slaves, God's first plague of turning the Nile to blood (Exodus 7:14-24) was a graphic reminder of Pharaoh's heinous scheme. And the final plague, the death of the firstborn sons in Egypt (Exodus 11), echoed the grief that had filled the land of Goshen nearly a century before.

When Jochebed gave birth to a son, she was determined to protect him. The family constructed a little floating basket of reeds and tar, placed the baby Moses into the basket, and set it afloat on the Nile. Ironically, the source of death for other sons became the avenue of life for Moses.

It is at the water's edge that we meet his older sister, Miriam, who risked her life to save his. She had his back. Following at a distance she watched as the tiny basket floated down to where the Egyptian princess was bathing. The baby Moses cried and attracted the princess to this tiny ark of salvation. She opened the basket and was overwhelmed with empathy for the helpless child.

Miriam's timing was perfect; she stepped out of the bushes along the bank and offered to find a Hebrew woman to nurse the infant. It took an extreme amount of courage for this slave girl to step openly into the presence of royalty. To walk into the private bathing area of Pharaoh's daughter certainly put her life at risk. Surely there would have been guards nearby who could have been summoned to the princess's aid. Miriam might have been killed on the spot for her audacious act, but the providence of God was at work.

Pharaoh's daughter seemed genuinely grateful for the offer and sent Miriam off on her quest. Miriam brought back her own mother, Jochebed, to the princess. What's more, the princess said, "Take this baby and nurse him for me, and I will pay you" (Exodus 2:9). God is good. In the midst of Goshen's tragedy, Jochebed nursed her own son—and got paid to do it! Such an offer would cheer up even the most disheartened mother.

It appears the princess realized that motherhood is a *big* job—and she didn't even have salary.com for reference! According to that site, if a mother were paid for the ten basic jobs she performs (housekeeper, day-care center teacher, cook, computer operator, laundry machine operator, janitor, facilities manager, van driver, psychologist, and CEO), her annual income would be $138,095.[2] We don't know what royal compensation Jochebed received, but at least she was paid!

Not every day has such a happy ending. One evening at home our daughter Rebekah got in trouble for misbehaving. We had been unaware that she'd already had a *tough* day in second grade—until later that night when this handwritten note appeared on my desk:

> Dad,
>
> I'm not sorry. It's been the worst day of my whole life, I got in a fight with Sarah. I got a minuse one on my spelling test. And I punched my cheek on aksident and it hert. And mom got mad at me. I have to take the spelling test all over. And I lost my nickle for snack money. The food wasn't good at lunch today.
>
> It has been a terribble horrible no good very bad day.
>
> From,
> ???

It wasn't too difficult to figure out who ??? was—or to guess the inspiration for Rebekah's note. We had recently read Judith Viorst's book *Alexander and the Terrible, Horrible, No Good, Very Bad Day*. All things considered, for a seven-year-old it had been a demoralizing day. Can you relate?

Not every day ends pleasantly. Though we celebrate the victory in Moses' household, there were thousands of slave homes where God did not intervene. Those good families endured the tragedy imposed by a cruel monarch. We dare not forget that we live in a broken world. God has never promised to right every wrong; to change every tragedy into triumph; or to miraculously spare us from hurt, pain, disease, and injustice. Not in this world! That's why family is so important—we need to be there for each other. In the tough moments of life, you need someone in the family to say, "Don't worry; I've got your back." When that happens, you know you are not alone in your struggles and that you will survive.

Miriam played a critical role in the preservation of her brother's life. She had his back. Obviously, the infant Moses had no idea at the time that he had a sister, let alone that she had just put her life on the line for him. Once he learned, he never forgot—and the day would come when he returned the favor.

This principle of being there for each other also applies to the church. We need to be there for one another in the body of Christ. Many among us do not have physical family close or available to help in time of need. The church may be our *only* family. According to the U.S. Census Bureau, since the beginning of the twenty-first century, an average of more than forty million people have moved annually.[3] Obviously, some of those moves are simply to a different house in the same area, but millions move away from family and familiar surroundings every year.

Today countless communities are temporarily home to international guests. Some come from north or south of U.S. borders; others come from different continents. Regardless of their point of origin, when they arrive in our hometowns, they are alone. If you have ever traveled to another culture, you know how uncomfortable it can be. The church has a wonderful opportunity to reach out to these "cultural orphans" and adopt them into the culture of the church. Through such efforts you not only will help them feel at home in your community, but more importantly, you will also have the opportunity to help them discover a relationship with Jesus Christ.

The church is a family. Isn't it great to know that we have siblings in the faith who will come alongside us in life's toughest moments and say, "Don't worry; I've got your back"? I am always encouraged when I hear about a small group that circles the wagons around the one in their group who is hurting. They call, take in food, help with the kids, mow the grass . . . In short, they do what a family does.

A few years ago our church leadership did a study on the biblical role of deacons. We concluded that the best current description for a deacon is that of a social worker or caregiver in the body of Christ. If one concludes that Acts 6:1-6 records the advent of the deacon's role, then working with and caring for those in need within the family of God is of paramount importance. The deacons at our church, Sherwood Oaks Christian, are individually assigned to a widow, widower, or family with needs.

I remember one widow in our congregation who had been left with no immediate family when her husband died. Her assigned deacon, Jeff, made a huge difference in her quality of life during her last years in this world. He and his family took extra interest in her, brought her to worship services on Sunday, and invited her to their home for special occasions. Jeff helped manage her meager finances and assisted with her chronic medical requirements. He spent hours ministering to the needs of this widow, who was basically unknown to most in the congregation. I am convinced that this widow lived longer and far better because of Jeff and his family.

Perhaps a deacon's role is characterized by the slogan "Don't worry; I've got your back."

WE'RE IN THIS TOGETHER, SO LET ME GIVE YOU A HAND

Many years after the exodus, the prophet Micah wrote, "I brought you up out of Egypt and redeemed you from the land of slavery. I sent Moses to lead you, *also Aaron and Miriam*" (Micah 6:4, emphasis added).

Although Moses is the most well known, he wasn't alone. His brother, Aaron, and sister, Miriam, were divinely appointed help. Together they were a team. Family doesn't just protect and watch over one another like Miriam did one day along the banks of the Nile—family lends a continuous helping hand. Being part of a family should be a wonderful blessing; in the family there exists a bond that strengthens and encourages.

Here's a fun assignment: First, list all the ways your family has helped you through the years. (You will not be graded on this!) Secondly, and more importantly, list the ways that *you* can be helpful to your family. (You *may* be graded on this one—God has instructed us to help one another.)

Not long ago I noted the various "one another" commands found in the New Testament. This is by no means an exhaustive list, but it does provide a glimpse into the priority that God places on helping one another. These "one anothers" reinforce so well the idea of "We're in this together, so let me give you a hand." And maybe they're also God's way of saying, "Play nice!"

- *Love one another deeply, from the heart. (This one is mentioned at least ten times.)*

- *Be devoted to one another.*

- *Honor one another.*

- *Live in harmony with one another.*

- *Don't pass judgment on one another.*

- *Accept one another.*

- *Instruct one another.*

- *Greet one another.*

- *Serve one another.*

- *Be patient with one another.*

- *Bear with one another.*

- *Be kind and compassionate to one another.*

- *Speak to one another with psalms.*

- *Submit to one another.*

- *Forgive one another.*

- *Admonish one another.*

o *Encourage one another.*

o *Don't hate one another.*

o *Spur one another on to good deeds.*

o *Be humble toward one another.*

o *Be hospitable to one another without grumbling.*

o *Have fellowship with one another.*

If you have your Father's eyes (and you do!), look for ways to encourage, support, or lend a helping hand to another in the family. Make a phone call or send a text message. Write an encouraging note or send an e-mail. Go for a face-to-face visit. Help with a home-improvement project. Get creative. You know what your family—the spiritual one as well as the physical one—needs from you, so just do it.

Remember, we're in this together! The older I get, the more I realize how every aspect of family provides value: parents, siblings, cousins, uncles, aunts, and in-laws. Yes, you heard right—in-laws.

A young lady came home from a date in tears. When her mother inquired about her sad disposition, the young lady responded with halting voice, "Alfred *(sob)* proposed to me *(sob)* an hour ago."

"That's wonderful, dear," her mother gushed. "So why are you disappointed?"

"Because *(more sobs)* he also told me he's an atheist. Oh Mom, he doesn't even believe there's a Hell."

"Marry him anyway, sweetheart," her mother responded. "Between the two of us, we'll show him how wrong he is."

For all our joking about in-laws, they truly are a blessing. We learn from them things we may have missed growing up in our own homes. We will see life from a different perspective when viewed through their eyes. We learn to consider the feelings of others when our clan swells to include those who enter via an "I do" and a thirty-dollar marriage certificate.

Moses' father-in-law was a real blessing to him. As the Israelites made their way from the banks of the Red Sea toward Canaan, Jethro came to Moses bringing Moses' wife, Zipporah, and their two sons (Exodus 18:1-8). It was a joyful meeting. (It's interesting that Moses customarily bowed and greeted Jethro with a kiss. The text offers nothing about how he greeted Zipporah, which may say a lot about their relationship!)

The day after the family reunion, Jethro accompanied Moses to his job. (I guess it was Take-Your-Father-in-Law-to-Work Day.) Jethro watched in stunned disbelief as Moses labored from morning until night solving the people's problems. As he witnessed his son-in-law trying to settle the disputes of the whole nation, he asked, "What is this you are doing?" (v. 14). Good question. Undoubtedly, Moses was a great leader—bold, courageous, highly spiritual . . . definitely the right man for the job. Additionally, he was the humblest man on earth (Numbers 12:3). He just wasn't gifted at delegation. From his father-in-law he learned the art of sharing the load. That wise counsel from Jethro may have saved Moses' sanity; it certainly helped speed up the process of hearing disputes so that everyone profited from the advice.

Many households today are blended families—they're not the traditional Norman Rockwell painting. Seventy-six-year-old Bill Baker of London wed Edna Harvey. Edna happened to be Bill's granddaughter's husband's mother or, to put it another way, his granddaughter's mother-in-law. That's where the confusion began, according to Bill's granddaughter, Lynn. She tried to explain the new arrangement in these terms: "My mother-in-law is now my stepgrandmother. My grandfather is now my stepfather-in-law. My mom is my sister-in-law and my brother is my nephew. But even crazier is that I'm now married to my uncle and my own children are my cousins."[4]

Each year 500,000 adults become new stepparents; each day 1,300 stepfamilies are formed. Today some 6.4 million children live with one birth parent and one stepparent. One in three Americans is now a stepparent, a stepchild, a stepsibling, or some other member of a stepfamily.[5] Before too long, blended families will outnumber traditional families. The challenges are great. It takes a strong commitment to family unity, as well as a Christ-centered focus, to make it work. If you are part of a blended family, you may be tempted to think of your family as less than ideal. Please don't. You have the opportunity to make a great family together. Work at it, pray for it, and stick together by helping each other through the tough times. Play nice!

The church is one big, blended family. It certainly requires effort to live harmoniously with everyone in the body of Christ; but since we have the same Father, we owe it to him to get along with one another. After all, we are family! We are in this together, so let's love one another and lend a helping hand.

LET'S PARTY!

I love a family party. After the freed Israelites crossed through the Red Sea and the Egyptian army perished in the sea, it was party time—and Miriam helped organize it on the banks. Once and for all they were free, and no one could take them back. This may have been the first time the former captives truly realized the magnitude of what God had done for them. Miriam took a tambourine and led the women in a celebration of joy. "Miriam sang to them: 'Sing to the LORD, for he is highly exalted. The horse and its rider he has hurled into the sea'" (Exodus 15:21).

We are quick to pray in times of crisis but slow to celebrate the magnitude of God's blessings. Miriam's example is a reminder that families should get together for good times as well as the sad times.

Michael Landon directed the television series *Little House on the Prairie* for nine seasons. The sixth episode of season one is a classic.[6] A Walnut Grove widow, Miss Amy, was about to celebrate her eightieth birthday, but she feared none of her children would come home for her party. One of her sons had been gone for fifteen years. To ensure they would come, Miss Amy enlisted the help of Doc Baker and the Ingalls family to fake her own death.

Sure enough, her children showed up for the funeral. Miss Amy stood quietly at the back of the church and listened to the kind things they said about her. Finally, she could stand it no longer. She removed her black veil, shocking the crowd that she was still alive. The scene ends with a truly happy birthday celebration.

That episode was entitled "If I Should Wake Before I Die." Perhaps we would do well to wake up before we die and celebrate the blessings of God with our families. Sorrows will dictate our actions if we aren't careful. But life is filled with far more joy than tears, so let's party!

A party can be as much an expression of worship as prayer can. The holy days of the Old Testament usually included a celebration in addition to the worship. If we love a party and if we have been created in the image of God, then what does that say about God's celebrative nature?

Perhaps we have unwittingly done a disservice to our children when we've made them think of worship as something serious and dull, something not fun. If the sermon is uninspiring and the congregants are somber, have we made God seem boring? It is important that our children witness genuine worship that's relevant, life changing, and exciting. The corporate worship of the church is vital to their spiritual health. But it certainly should not be the only worship they experience.

Personal worship needs to be seen at home—around the dinner table, out in the backyard . . . And personal reverence can be expressed to God through helping a neighbor, going the extra mile, being sacrificial with time and resources, or celebrating the good moments that are gifts from God. Teach your family to worship every day in every way—it is a necessary tool for their survival.

I FORGIVE YOU

It finally happened—a family squabble erupted between Miriam and Moses. After Zipporah died Moses married again, and this time he married a Cushite woman whose heritage was Ethiopian. Miriam lost her spiritual perspective and allowed the jealousy of human nature to take over. True, this new wife was not of Jewish birth, but the problem may have been larger than heritage. Maybe sibling rivalry was at work here. Miriam might have been jealous of Moses because she herself never married. Or perhaps she resented this new wife who was taking Moses' attention away from their brother-sister relationship.

Regardless of the motive, Miriam incited Aaron to join her in this family feud, and they both spoke out against Moses. Numbers 12:1, 2 records these words: "Miriam and Aaron began to talk against Moses because of his Cushite wife. . . . 'Has the LORD spoken only through Moses?' they asked. 'Hasn't he also spoken through us?' And the LORD heard this."

Sibling rivalry is not limited to kids; adults sometimes suffer with it more. It begins innocently enough in children—the pulling of hair or the unwillingness to share a prized toy—but left unchecked it may result in permanent enmity between adult siblings.

It's an old problem. Adam and Eve never had in-law issues, but they *did* lose a son to sibling rivalry.

God was so angry with Miriam for speaking against his servant Moses that he struck her with deadly leprosy. Moses didn't respond with, "Serves you right, sis. That'll teach you to say mean things about me!" He immediately responded with intercessory prayer. This is the moment when Moses paid his debt to Miriam for saving his infant life. God graciously answered Moses' prayers and reduced the death sentence to only a week of leprosy and isolation outside the camp of Israel (vv. 10-15).

The Israelites had earlier seen the radiant face of Moses, but at this moment it was his character that shone brightly. He wasn't perfect—he was guilty of sin and had committed his fair share of mistakes—but he exhibited three terrific qualities:

o   *He was quick to forgive.*

o   *He was quick to pray.*

o   *He was quick to restore.*

What a model for family harmony! If you will practice those principles inside your family circle, it will transform your home. Genuine forgiveness is a hallmark of a Christ-follower, a powerful force of reconciliation, and an example that always points others to Jesus. Learn to forgive and play nice—the world is watching.

Growing up as a sibling can be challenging in both the home and the church. We owe it to one another to make the process as pleasant as possible.

o   *Watch over your family—there are rough waters to navigate.*

o   *Stand by your family—they will need someone to lean on in the painful moments of life.*

o   *Instruct your family—your wisdom may ease their stress.*

o   *Encourage your family—discouragement, like a hungry crocodile on the banks of the Nile, lurks around every bend, waiting to devour your family's joy.*

o   *Love your family—no one can care for them more than you do.*

Life beyond your backyard will introduce your family to hatred, prejudice, dishonesty, disappointment, rejection, anger, fear, and bitterness. No wonder your family longs to hear these words:

o   *Don't worry; I've got your back.*

o   *We're in this together, so let me give you a hand.*

o   *Let's party!*

o   *I forgive you.*

1 Only ten crewmen of the USS *Juneau* were rescued, but the survivors had no difficulty remembering the Sullivan boys' motto: "We stick together!" That's what families do. They stick together—in good times and bad, in the fun moments as well as the sad.

How does your family stick together? What action plan can you devise that will help encourage such support?

2 We dare not forget that we live in a broken world. God has never promised to right every wrong; to change every tragedy into triumph; or to miraculously spare us from hurt, pain, disease, and injustice. Not in this world! That's why family is so important—we need to be there for each other.

Specifically, what can you do in your family to ease the pain of a broken world? How can the church as a family address the hurt, pain, and injustice in this world? How can you be available to help others when life's injustices leave them empty?

3 Your family longs to hear these words:

- Don't worry; I've got your back.
- We're in this together, so let me give you a hand.
- Let's party!
- I forgive you.

How do these expressions encourage members of the family? Do your actions in your family back up your words? Which of these expressions is the most important one of all? Why?

4 First, list all the ways your family has helped you through the years. . . . Secondly, and more importantly, list the ways that *you* can be helpful to your family.

Remember to complete this assignment if you didn't do it earlier.

The only way to have a friend is to be one.
RALPH WALDO EMERSON

In elementary school my best friend was Randy Emerson. I couldn't imagine having a better friend. We played at each other's homes, were in the same Cub Scout troop, and even had a crush on the same girl in third grade and thought that was pretty cool. Then one day Randy told me his family was moving. That's all that registered. I didn't hear where or why—I just felt this emptiness in the pit of my stomach. I was losing my best friend.

Elementary school boys have good intentions, but we didn't stay in touch. Gone was a connection in my life that really mattered.

Sunny Schaeuble and our daughter Emily have been inseparable since elementary school. Having been born just a day apart, they seemed destined to be best friends from the beginning. The two share the same values, loyalty, and strong faith in Christ. Their hearts seem to beat as one. Their friendship has been an answer to our prayers as parents.

Sometimes they laughed together until they cried; sometimes they cried together until they laughed again. College took them in different directions; but even now, when they get together it's as if they have never been apart. I remember when the girls went on an out-of-state trip to an amusement park with their middle school class. Both were excited, but neither would have gone without the other. It was all or nothing with those two. Their relationship captures the essence of Solomon's wisdom: "There are 'friends' who destroy each other, but a real friend sticks closer than a brother" (Proverbs 18:24, *NLT*). Such loyalty is the foundation of lasting friendships.

Most people long for personal connections. Have you noticed that hermits and recluses do not make up the bulk of society? Why aren't more of us self-sufficient loners? Because God didn't wire us that way. He created us for friendship. The Lone Ranger had Tonto, Sheriff Andy Taylor had Deputy Barney Fife, Jerry Seinfeld had Kramer, and Homer Simpson had . . . oops, wrong list. In reality, we want to build friendships like the one shared by Sunny and Emily.

Personal connections are important. It's not *what* you know but *who* you know that matters. You cheer from a seat on the fifty-yard line at an NFL play-off game because your friend has an extra ticket. You meet the girl of your dreams because your friend introduces you to her. You fly free to the Bahamas for an exotic vacation because your friend works for the airline. See? It's who you know. Personal connections matter.

When you eat out, which server gets the best tip? The one who makes a personal connection with you. Which doctor will you wait hours to see? The one who makes a personal connection with you. Which teacher is at the top of your list of favorites? The one who makes a personal connection with you.

May I be so bold as to suggest that your personal connections and friendships will change your life? While you're chewing on that thought, let's meet one of the richest men Jesus ever encountered.

FOUR FAITHFUL FRIENDS

He lived along the Sea of Galilee in the quaint fishing community of Capernaum—home to Peter, Andrew, James, and John. This rich man may have been a fisherman at one time, but not at the time of our story. As a matter of fact, his life had taken a demoralizing downward turn; because he had become paralyzed, he couldn't do any of the things he longed to do. He had lost his independence. Benevolence was likely the only means of support for his family, but even then he was dependent upon others to physically move him to a high-traffic area. He couldn't even beg alone.

I can't begin to imagine what it would be like to be paralyzed. Have you ever stumbled out of bed when the interrupted flow of blood caused your leg to go numb? It's an odd sensation to lose the momentary control and feeling of a limb, but to *never* have any feeling or control is difficult to comprehend. Imagine the emotions and attitudes that accompany paralysis: fear, loneliness, embarrassment, anger, bitterness, uselessness, inadequacy, frustration, and impatience. The list is long. So are the days when you cannot move on your own power. Maintaining one's sanity could be a daily battle.

I'm speculating (since the Bible is silent about this) that, despite his circumstances, this rich man had demonstrated a positive attitude throughout his life. He had four buddies who seemed to take a great interest in his well-being. Grouchy, negative people seldom have many faithful friends; eventually the negativity drives them away. But this man had endeared himself to four very resourceful guys. Perhaps these were the men who took him to beg in the morning and brought him back home each evening. I suspect he teased them or had a new joke each day when they came to pick him up . . . *literally*. I wonder if his sense of humor kept them laughing or if his genuine sense of gratitude kept them encouraged. I just have a feeling they would have gone anywhere and done anything to help this friend. And one day that's exactly what happened.

The news was out: Jesus of Nazareth was back in town, and he was preaching in one of the local houses, probably Peter's. A crowd had squeezed itself into the fisherman's home, filling every nook and cranny. Those who couldn't get in crowded around windows and doors outside, hoping to get a peek. Packed sardines in mustard sauce have more room than the people who were intent on hearing Jesus speak that day.

The quintet arrived a bit too late to get a front-row seat. For that matter, they couldn't even attract Jesus' attention from the doorway. But these four guys had been waiting too long for this special moment—they weren't about to give up. Undaunted, they headed for the outside stairway to the roof. And once on the roof, they began to dig through the clay, straw, and limbs that comprised the roofing material. Unprepared for this task, they resorted to using their bare hands and fishermen's knives.

UNFORGETTABLE

This whole ordeal must have been very distracting for those trying to concentrate on the message. As a preacher I know it doesn't take much to distract a listener, but let the roof cave in . . . and *I'm* going to be distracted too!

I was still a teenager when I preached for an evening service at the Troy Christian Church in southern Indiana. I was nervous to begin with; then about a third of the way into my sermon, I heard a creaking, rumbling sort of sound. Without further warning, the ceiling tiles in the back of the church gave way and water cascaded out of the hole—enough to fill a washtub!

Nobody was aware until that soggy moment that rainwater had been collecting in the leaky belfry. Needless to say, I lost the audience. I too stood there dumbfounded—how was I supposed to know the congregation had gone from immersion to pouring! To this day whenever I see the good folks from Troy, they remind me of the night that something other than bats came flying out of their belfry. Some church services are simply unforgettable.

The service in Capernaum that day was unforgettable. The house was uncomfortably hot—it was packed with sweaty people who smelled of fish, the windows and doorways were blocked with other sweaty listeners, and there was no circulation. Whew, it must have been stifling! Add to the sticky, humid atmosphere swirling dust and chunks of dirt falling from the ceiling, and you've got the perfect recipe for room rage! The boys above didn't give up despite the angry looks from below. They tore away the ceiling until they had a hole large enough to lower their slightly embarrassed, paralyzed pal.

With halting motion they winched him down until he was suspended right in front of Jesus. I'm confident the crowd didn't enjoy any of this, but Jesus sure did. What an expression of faith!

If you think the hole in the roof was a surprise, wait until you hear what Jesus did. Looking compassionately at the man lowered before him, he proclaimed, "Son, your sins are forgiven" (Mark 2:5). What! Forgiven? Everyone's expressions changed in reaction to that statement:

o   *The religious leaders' faces registered anger; to them his words were blasphemous. Only God could forgive sin!*

o   *The faces among the crowd indicated confusion; to them his words made no sense. Even they could tell the man had come for healing.*

o   *The four faces peering down from above suggested disappointment; to them his words were empty and hopeless. They had worked so hard getting their friend to Jesus for physical healing that they missed what the depth of this spiritual cleansing would mean.*

o   *The face from the mat signified joy; how could it be anything less when looking into the eyes of God?*

Reading the minds of the religiously educated, Jesus scolded them for doubtful thoughts. He then posed this question: "Which is easier: to say, 'Your sins are forgiven,' or to say, 'Get up and walk'?" (Luke 5:23). Obviously, it is much easier to promise forgiveness. Such a statement cannot be dismissed or confirmed by any outward evidence. But to command a paralyzed man to get up and walk is an entirely different story. If the man can't respond to such a command, the would-be healer's credibility is forever destroyed.

To prove he had the power to forgive, Jesus also restored the man's ability to walk. There were no atrophied muscles to limit his movement. No physical therapist was ushered in to provide treatment. The man stood up, picked up his mat, and moved toward the door. Funny, isn't it? The crowd wouldn't let him in, but they sure made room for him to walk out! Seeing God at work has a way of changing your perspective. Even the skeptics were amazed.

You may be wondering why I described the paralyzed man as rich when in reality he probably had very little money. Simple. He met Jesus face-to-face, had his sins forgiven, was healed of his paralysis, and had four of the best friends in the world. Any man who has all that is rich beyond description!

Do you feel a twinge of envy when you read this story? Do you find yourself pondering, *Why can't I have four friends like that?* Most people would pay good money to have such loyal buddies—roof-crashin' friends—but of course, true relationships can't be bought.

The more important question to ask is: "Why can't I *be* a friend like that?" The good news is that you can! You just need to be intentional about that goal. Some subtle shifts in thinking will get us moving in a friendly direction.

LOOK FOR A MEANS TO CONNECT

I wish we knew the connection between those five friends. What was it that created such a strong bond between them? It could have been any of a number of different things. Perhaps they had been fishing partners at one time. Maybe they all were the same age and had studied together. Maybe these five had married five sisters. Maybe they enjoyed going to the coliseum (packing fish sandwiches and kosher pickles) to watch the Bethlehem Rams face off against the Capernaum Anglers.

This I *do* know: friendships seldom develop between people who never find a bond. In building relationships with others, we need to look for connecting points. Here are a few examples.

AGE

People of a similar age or at a similar life stage generally connect easily because they share so much from a common period of time: music, clothing styles, first cars, third-grade teachers, favorite movies, college experiences, infamous news stories, and military service, to name a few. They can compare notes on raising children, health concerns, and retirement planning. Age is a good connecting point.

LOCALITY

Have you ever been traveling on vacation and met someone from your hometown? You probably felt an immediate connection.

In the early days of our nation, immigrants often migrated to similar areas. For instance, immigrants from Scandinavian countries settled in the states of Wisconsin and Minnesota because the terrain and climate reminded them of home. In many large metropolitan areas, sections of the city became known as Chinatown, Little Italy, the Polish Quarter, and so forth. Locality can be a good connecting point.

HOBBIES AND INTERESTS

When I meet someone who enjoys antique cars or aviation as much as I do, I don't have to know him well to feel an immediate connection. Conversation comes easily, and willingness to help out with a project is a given. Think about what you enjoy doing in your spare time, and count how many friends you have who enjoy the same things.

SUFFERING

It really is true that misery loves company. Suffering people often gravitate toward others who have experienced or are experiencing a similar trial. Widows enjoy the company of other women who have lost their husbands. Cancer patients connect with those who have endured chemo or radiation treatments. Struggling parents long to hear how other parents adjust to having an estranged teen.

Take inventory of what you enjoy doing, where you've been, and what you've experienced. It may be those very characteristics that will help you connect with someone else who desperately needs you to be a friend.

And when you *become* a friend, you will *have* a friend.

LOOK FOR A NEED TO MEET

This *should* be easy. Everybody has needs, and yet those needs so often go unmet. The problem isn't finding a need to meet; it's taking the time to look. I don't ever finish my to-do list. I seem to have more than I can get done in one lifetime. Consequently, I don't often take the time to look for the needs of others. Unless they are made obvious, I can easily overlook them. We must become intentional about *looking* for needs to meet.

How many needs do you find in this account from the Gospels? The need of the paralyzed man was obvious—he needed healing. But there were other needs in that packed house that we often overlook, some of which were far more critical than his.

o *The crowd was willing to tolerate the hot and uncomfortable conditions in that house. Why? Why not wait for another occasion to hear Jesus? Because that crowd was desperately searching for God. They needed courage to face their fears, they needed answers for their daily problems, and they needed hope in order to not give up. They needed God and found him in Jesus.*

o *The four friends needed affirmation for their actions. They had seriously damaged someone's roof in an effort to help their friend. They wanted to know that their vandalism had been worth the risk.*

o *The teachers of the law were in danger of missing the opportunity of a lifetime. They were so blinded by their interpretations of the law that they had missed the lawgiver himself. They needed spiritual sight to see the truth.*

Yes, there were multiple needs in the house that day, but we miss most of them because of the excitement of the paralyzed man's encounter with Jesus. It is not much different today. We miss so many needs because we tend to see only the big or apparent ones. Start looking for the less obvious needs around you. Meeting those can be every bit as rewarding as meeting what appears to be a grander need.

I am often overwhelmed by the needs of people in my own backyard. Not a week goes by that I don't learn about some disheartening struggle:

o *parents watching their child die with inoperable cancer*

o *children whose aging parent has just been diagnosed with Alzheimer's* o   *a young man battling ALS (Lou Gehrig's disease)*

o   *a father who has a massive heart attack and leaves a young family behind*

o   *a recent retiree, just ready to enjoy his free time, suffers a debilitating stroke*

The list seems endless. I know of marriages that are hanging by a thread, parents who are ready to throw in the towel, and teens who are starving for their parents' approval. Jobs are lost, retirements are squandered, dreams are crushed . . . The next crisis is right around the corner. Just open your eyes—the needs are staggering. In the crisis moments, most people desperately need a friend to help keep them grounded and focused on Jesus Christ. The paralyzed man needed friends to lower him down; most people need a friend to pull them up.

LOOK FOR A WAY TO ENCOURAGE

When I read about the four men who carried their paralyzed friend to Jesus and then worked their fingers to the bone to get him a front-row seat, I think it's safe to conclude that they were encouragers. I'm convinced that had their mission failed, it still would have been a day well spent. The man couldn't help but be encouraged by such a wonderful scheme and four wonderful friends. In a world full of discouraging experiences and empty promises, it's refreshing to meet an encourager.

When I was a kid, I had an inflatable punching bag that looked like a clown. I could push it, plow into it, or punch it (the nose squeaked); but it always righted itself. How? The rounded bottom of the bag was filled with sand, which served as a ballast to keep it stable.

May I suggest that an encourager is the sand in the bottom of a punching bag? If we live long enough, we will be pushed, punched, pummeled, and plowed into. Disappointments and tough circumstances work overtime to keep people down, but I believe God wants us to be like the sand in the bottom of the bag—no matter how often those around us fall over, we keep helping them back up. Nineteenth-century philosopher Johann Goethe wrote, "Correction does much, but encouragement does more."[1] I like the way Ella Wheeler Wilcox said the same thing: "A pat on the back is only a few vertebrae removed from a kick in the pants, but is miles ahead in results."[2] Just like the four roof crashers, a friend encourages people by getting them back on their feet again.

Up into her late nineties, my grandmother Ellsworth wrote to me weekly, and in each letter she included a single dollar bill. She often wrote about people I didn't know or events I couldn't quite figure out. Sometimes I couldn't even read her writing. But it didn't matter; just getting her letter was special.

Grandma took some pretty hard knocks in her life, but by God's grace she kept bouncing back. Perhaps it was through those tough times that she learned to be such a good encourager. She has been at home with the Lord for several years now. I miss her, her letters . . . and the dollars! Through her words and actions, she modeled how to be an encourager, the sand at the bottom that keeps bringing people back to the top.

LOOK FOR AN OPPORTUNITY TO BE LIKE JESUS

Proverbs 17:17 says, "A friend loves at all times." Looking at the life of Jesus, it is apparent that he viewed being a friend as important. He was a friend to children—they seemed to flock to him. He addressed his disciples as friends. The Jewish leaders accused him of being "a friend of tax collectors and 'sinners'" (Matthew 11:19), an accusation Jesus never refuted. Though he would momentarily raise Lazarus to life, Jesus still wept at the tomb of his dear friend. Even when Jesus' betrayer, Judas, approached him with the kiss of death, Jesus responded, "Friend, do what you came for" (Matthew 26:50).

Of all the Scriptures about friends, nothing compares to these words of Jesus on the night before his crucifixion: "Greater love has no one than this, that he lay down his life for his friends. You are my friends if you do what I command. I no longer call you servants, because a servant does not know his master's business. Instead, I have called you friends" (John 15:13-15).

The secret to being a good friend lies in emulating Jesus' selfless attitude toward reaching out to friends. Dave Sears is actively involved in the life of our congregation and is a friend to many. In 2004 he saw a television program that chronicled the difficult journey of Larry Alford, who lost his left arm in a car accident. Larry, having been on the college golf team (he once played against Tiger Woods), had always dreamed of pursuing a career in professional golf, but the accident changed all that . . . sort of.

Larry's stepfather created a prosthetic arm that allowed him to hit a golf ball; his dream wasn't dead yet. But just when things were looking up, Larry's car was stolen. That's not the worst part. Since his "arm" was in the backseat, he lost that too. Larry was devastated. A surgeon created a new arm for him, but Larry had no financial means to purchase it.

The story touched a nerve with Dave; he saw the program more than once and couldn't get Larry out of his mind. At the end of the program, the network flashed Larry's Web site on the screen, and Dave logged on. Finding Larry's phone number listed there, Dave called. He told Larry he would pay for the arm.

Dave didn't know it when he placed the call, but Larry related that it had been one of the worst days of his life. He had just finished praying for some kind of assistance when his phone rang.

Today Larry's dream has come true—maybe not as he had first envisioned it, but I'm quite certain he would tell you it's even better than he thought possible. Larry and Dave have forged a friendship, but that's not all; they are also forming a foundation that will help others in need. Larry is spending his life on the golf course, conducting charity golf tournaments all across the country. Not only does he openly share his faith in Christ, he points to Dave as the friend who made his dream a reality.

In his quiet way, Dave continues to be more concerned about *being* a friend than *having* one. Nearly every week Dave tells me about some new people-project he's discovered. Whether in our congregation or halfway across the country, he continually looks for ways to connect with those who have needs. Without fanfare he then meets those needs in his encouraging manner. Every day Dave Sears looks for an opportunity to be like Jesus. Shouldn't we all?

I had just uttered the benediction one Sunday morning and was walking up the center aisle, shaking hands with some of our members who were still awake. I felt a tap on my shoulder and turned to extend my hand to a fifty-two-year-old man who said, "Hi, Tom. I'm Randy Emerson." For a moment I was speechless. (I know it's hard to believe of a preacher.)

There, after nearly forty years, stood my best friend from elementary school. Memories flooded my mind; and though my tongue was silent, my arms knew what to do. We exchanged a bear hug, and then he introduced me to his wife, Leslie. For the few minutes between services, we visited nonstop. After they left I thought of dozens of questions I should have asked, but this time I knew where to find Randy. I lost that connection once; I don't ever want to lose it again.

When sin slithered into God's beautiful backyard garden and marred his perfect creation, our bond with the Father was destroyed. But at Calvary

God shouted across the ages, "I lost that connection once; I don't ever want to lose it again." No wonder Jesus said, "Greater love has no one than this, that he lay down his life for his friends." I encourage you to become a friend to someone in need in your own backyard . . . or beyond. Your faithful friendship—roof-crashin' friendship—may be the very thing to bring that person closer in friendship with Jesus.

1 Having been born just a day apart, they seemed destined to be best friends from the beginning. The two share the same values, loyalty, and strong faith in Christ.

Have you ever had a friendship like that? What are the qualities you look for in a friend?

2 They tore away the ceiling until they had a hole large enough to lower their slightly embarrassed, paralyzed pal. With halting motion they winched him down until he was suspended right in front of Jesus. I'm confident the crowd didn't enjoy any of this, but Jesus sure did. What an expression of faith!

We can certainly understand how desperate these men were to get their friend to Jesus. How far would you go to help a friend in need? What are some practical ways in which you connect with those in need?

3 Jobs are lost, retirements are squandered, dreams are crushed . . . The next crisis is right around the corner. Just open your eyes—the needs are staggering.

What are some specific ways in which you can be an encourager to those who are facing tough times? Think about those who are right in your backyard. How can you be "a friend who sticks closer than a brother" (Proverbs 18:24)?

4 Looking at the life of Jesus, it is apparent that he viewed being a friend as important. He was a friend to children—they seemed to flock to him. He addressed his disciples as friends. The Jewish leaders accused him of being "a friend of tax collectors and 'sinners'" (Matthew 11:19), an accusation Jesus never refuted.

Jesus was a model of true friendship. What qualities do you see in Jesus that would make you a good friend? How can you begin to look at others as Jesus did and see them as potential friends?

It's not true that nice guys finish last. Nice guys are winners before the game even starts.
ADDISON WALKER

As a kid I thought we had only six neighbors. I reasoned that since the yards of these families bordered our yard at some point, they fit the definition. I never worried about their being upset when I walked through their yards—we were neighbors. I wouldn't have hesitated a moment to ask them for help—we were neighbors. Steve's backyard bordered my backyard, so it just made sense to be best friends—we were neighbors. Even when my dog came home dragging the Schneiders' Christmas ham, we remained friends—after all, we were neighbors. (And yes, we replaced the ham.)

I realize the theology of my early years was a little weak. OK, a *lot* weak—but I suspect I wasn't alone in my understanding. Most people think of a neighbor as the person next door, but not all border residents necessarily make *good* neighbors. We have a physician friend who once lived next door to a family that was impossible to please. They complained about everything! It got so bad that Doc's family started calling them "the neighbors from Hell." Ironically, they patronized our friend's clinic; that is, until the day the mother swore at the nursing staff. That was the last straw. Though their houses were separated only by a short distance, their values were worlds apart. They didn't feel like neighbors.

At one time we lived in a parsonage that was only a few feet from the house next door. The elderly lady who lived there took great joy in watching our activities through our windows. She gave us a daily review of the guests who had visited us. She reminded me of Gladys Kravitz, the nosy and obnoxious neighbor in the old TV series *Bewitched*.

Unfortunately, unlike Samantha, I couldn't twitch my nose and make our windows disappear!

Sometimes you find neighbors where you least expect them. One day I took my 1948 Chrysler to have the brakes replaced. On the way home, the car died in the middle of an intersection during rush hour. You don't have to be a brain surgeon to know that the quickest way to kindle road rage is to block an intersection when weary workers are trying to get home for supper. I hopped out of the car and started to push. Have you ever tried to push a 3,700-pound car through an intersection by yourself? Samson I am not. I began to feel the glare of the NASCAR wannabes. Any minute I expected to hear a symphony of irate horns. And though I didn't look up, I'm quite certain there were a few not-so-encouraging hand gestures.

Suddenly the car lurched forward. I looked back and there, pushing the car, was my daughter (who had been following me in her car), along with a man and woman I didn't know. The strangers didn't appear angry or indisposed; as a matter of fact, they acted like they were having fun with this. They thought the classic car was pretty cool. We pushed it a block and a half until we could get it off the road. Then as quickly as the man and woman had appeared, they were gone. I didn't find out who they were or where they were headed. I had never seen them before (and doubt that I will see them again), but in those few minutes they were neighbors to me. I needed help—desperately—and they came to my rescue! They were just out doin' good in the hood.

WHO IS MY NEIGHBOR?

If a neighbor can't be singled out by property lines or suburban housing additions, then how can he be identified? Exactly who *is* my neighbor? I'm not the first to ask that question; that query has a bit of age on it. One afternoon a Jewish scholar came to Jesus with another really important question. In his mind it had nothing to do with neighbors, but he would soon discover otherwise.

This expert in the law of Moses was more interested in traps than truth. What could he possibly learn from this unorthodox Galilean preacher? "Teacher," he began, "what must I do to inherit eternal life?"

Jesus responded, "You are the scholar, the expert. You tell me."

Experts are always ready and willing to talk. This one answered with the obvious; he quoted from the Shema, Deuteronomy 6:5, where the law teaches us to love God with heart, soul, mind, and strength. Or simply, love God with everything you are. But he didn't stop with the obvious; he added Leviticus 19:18: "Love your neighbor as yourself." It is not clear whether the scholar was simply repeating what he had been taught or if indeed he understood the powerful truth that loving one's neighbor *is* also a way of loving God. The two are difficult to separate.

On another occasion Jesus was questioned about the greatest commandment. The Lord quickly pointed out that the law of Moses and the prophets' writings rest on this very premise—love God, love others.

I suspect Jesus smiled when he said to the scholar, "You have answered correctly" (Luke 10:28). But before the man could bask in the warmth of this praise, Jesus added this postscript: "Now, go practice what you preach." Ouch! Suddenly, the accuser had become the accused. He'd been caught with his hand in the hypocrite's cookie jar. Apparently this expert had the facts but not the acts; he loved the creed but not the deed. Trying to salve his conscience and redeem his public image, he fired back, "And just who is my neighbor?"

No doubt, Jesus was waiting for that very opportunity. Luke 10:30 opens with an interesting word, which isn't conveyed in the *NIV*. It means that Jesus did more than merely reply. He "took up" the challenge laid down by this scholar; he jumped at the chance to drive home his point.

This lawyer should have quit while he was still behind! It's never wise to go toe-to-toe with the author of the words in question. The crowd was now deeply involved in the debate and hung on every word! What came next is one of Jesus' most memorable stories.

Going down to Jericho from Jerusalem was a treacherous undertaking. The elevation dropped over 3,500 feet as the road snaked its way to the town of Joshua's military fame. And since Joshua's day this trek had been known as Bloody Pass. Sounds like the title of an old Clint Eastwood Western, doesn't it? Anyone foolish enough to travel it alone deserved what he got. As the story unfolds, the inevitable has happened to our average Joe . . . or in this case, average Joseph; the roadside terrorists have taken their plunder and left him bloody, beaten, and near death.

The man needs help—in the worst way—and he knows he cannot survive long in his condition without assistance. Every little sound startles him as it echoes off the craggy heights. The lengthening shadows along the narrow, stony path taunt him as he peers out through swollen eyes to catch a glimpse of a would-be rescuer. Suddenly, he hears footsteps—brisk at first, but then they slow and finally stop nearby. He can't lift his head to make eye contact, but he can tell from the robe's fringe that it's a temple priest. Hallelujah! Help has arrived . . .

Silence.

Before the man could speak, the priest's feet stepped back and then hurried on more swiftly than before.

Growing weaker with every passing minute, the hurt man wondered if there would be others. His ears, keen to his surroundings, picked up another noise. Humming? It sounded like a song he had heard while in worship at the temple. Another priest perhaps? The humming stopped, and the injured man could hear the other man gasp. There was no pause this time. The worship assistant bolted from the scene as quickly as if someone had just entered the temple courts with a pig in tow.

The temperatures were falling, and so were the man's hopes. What a miserable way to die—stuck in the shadows on Bloody Pass with no one to help him get home. Would his family ever know the truth about what had happened? Would his widow and children have to glean from the corners of other farmers' fields because they had no one to provide for them? Would there be rumors that he had abandoned his family to run off with another woman from Jerusalem? The visions became even more haunting as his body grew weaker.

Suddenly more steps, another gasp . . . and then eyes that bent down to meet his. The greeting was spoken with kindness, but the accent was unmistakably Samaritan. *It's all over now,* he thought. *If only the priest or Levite had stopped, I might have had a fighting chance.* But at this point the man was too weak to resist. Maybe the Samaritan would just push him over the edge of the nearby cliff; that would be quick. He felt strong arms reach under his head and legs. Perhaps he tensed and began to pray softly, "God of Abraham, Isaac, and Jacob . . ." But his body was not moved in the direction of the cliff. Rather, he headed back into the sunlight.

Gently the Samaritan placed him in the middle of the road; the heat from the sun felt good on his cold body. Could it be that this disgrace of a man— if you could call a Samaritan a man—was actually trying to help him? He felt the sting of wine being poured into his open wounds, followed by the soothing warmth of olive oil. The Samaritan tore off part of his robe and made crude bandages for the worst of the cuts, and then, with an oil-soaked cloth, he gently wiped the matted blood from the sufferer's face. Once again the victim was lifted from the ground—and this time placed on the Samaritan's donkey. The three of them started down the road together. The rhythmic clomping of the donkey's hooves was comforting; and the farther they descended, the more the man's hopes rose.

The inn was a welcome oasis, and he had no trouble falling asleep. When he finally awoke he discovered that the Samaritan had not only paid the lodging expenses for both of them but had also promised the innkeeper he would pay whatever additional fees were needed until the victim was well enough to travel home.

Jesus may have paused here to let the story sink in, then posed this question: "Which of these three was a neighbor to the man who had been attacked?" (see Luke 10:36). I'm confident that at this point the scholar wished he had never even seen Jesus. There was no escape; the crowd anxiously awaited his answer. He couldn't bring himself to utter the word *Samaritan*, so he simply responded, "The merciful one." Again, I think Jesus smiled compassionately and said, "Go and do the same."

I realize there is a danger in making more of a parable than Jesus intended, but this story is rich in application. The heart of the issue isn't the *scholar's* question, but the *Savior's* question. It isn't about the who; it's about the how. Identifying those *who* qualify as neighbors isn't difficult; determining *how* I should be a neighbor is the challenge.

TAKING ON PREJUDICE

We love this story! It's filled with a sense of adventure, an unexpected response, and a happy ending. We also love it because it isn't so personal—we don't have issues with Samaritans. Jesus' Jewish audience certainly did! The crowd in Judea wasn't oohing and aahing with delight as they heard this story; they were squirming in their seats. Jesus pushed his listeners way out of their comfort zones with this parable; even his disciples were uncomfortable.

Do you need proof? As powerful as this story has been through the last twenty centuries, Luke is the only Gospel writer to include it in his narrative. It is incredible to note that neither Matthew nor Mark record *any* encounter with a Samaritan during the entire ministry of Jesus. And John mentions only one: the woman at the well (John 4). But Luke writes about three encounters:

o *On one occasion a Samaritan village was not receptive to a visit from Jesus. James and John were so indignant that they offered to call down fire from Heaven to destroy every last one of the village inhabitants (Luke 9:51-56). Talk about seeker sensitive!*

o *On another occasion Luke tells of Jesus' encounter with ten men on the border of Galilee and Samaria who had leprosy. They cried out for mercy and healing. Jesus simply told them to go show themselves to the priest. As they walked away they noticed their leprosy had miraculously disappeared. Words could not begin to express their incredible joy, but only one man returned to thank Jesus—and he was a Samaritan! (Luke 17:11-19).*

o *Luke alone records the fact that Jesus made a Samaritan the protagonist of one of his most powerful parables. We know it today as the Parable of the Good Samaritan, but no son of Abraham would ever have used* good *and* Samaritan *in the same breath. There was no such creature.*

Why did Luke include these Samaritan stories when no other writer did? Because Luke wasn't a Jew. As a Gentile Luke felt no bias or prejudice for the Samaritans. He had no dog in this fight.

Interestingly, the Jews and Samaritans *were* neighbors in the sense we usually mean. Samaria was sandwiched between Judea and Galilee; it bordered each of the Jewish territories. But the hatred was so intense that a devout Jew would avoid cutting through Samaria even though it was the quickest way from one region to the other.

Why such hatred? Nine hundred years before Jesus' parable, there were two Jewish states: the northern kingdom called Israel, whose capital was Samaria; and the southern kingdom called Judah, whose capital was Jerusalem. In 722 *BC*, the northern kingdom was conquered by the Assyrians. As with any conquest, some of the people were left behind as slave labor to work the land. The brightest and best were hauled off to the conqueror's capital. Second Kings 17 explains the root of the hatred: Though the city of Samaria was destroyed, those left behind married the idolatrous pagans from surrounding nations. As a result of the intermarriage, their faith in God was diluted. The nation of Judah viewed them as spiritual half-breeds. The hatred between the two groups only intensified as the years progressed. About a century before Jesus' birth, a band of Jews destroyed a Samaritan temple on Mount Gerizim; and sometime after the birth of Jesus, a group of Samaritans retaliated by scattering dead men's bones in the Jerusalem temple, desecrating it during the Passover celebration.[1]

It's no wonder this story met with such a cool reception, but Jesus was determined to prove that the love of God was greater than any prejudice. To demonstrate his point he changed the life of a Samaritan divorcée at a well, healed a Samaritan victim of leprosy in a border town, and cast the starring role in his parable to a Samaritan rescuer.

There is no room in God's kingdom for bias or prejudice. One color is not more desirable than another. One race is not more loved by God nor more needed in the church nor more anticipated in Heaven. It makes no difference whether you are black or white; male or female; rich or poor; formally educated or experience educated; handsome or homely; popular or unpopular; Republican, Democrat, independent, libertarian, or politically fed up! In this world we all would be lost without a Savior.

In the church we all are one because of his grace. In our communities we all are *neighbors*!

However, we are not above the conflict of these first-century Jews and Samaritans. What if this parable had originally been told in another time and place? Would we grasp the implications more clearly?

o   *During our American Civil War, it might have been an emancipated slave who stopped to rescue a slave trader.*

o   *In the hills of eastern Kentucky, it might have been a Hatfield who stopped to rescue a McCoy.*

o   *In war-torn Europe it might have been an escaping Jew who stopped to rescue a Nazi SS officer.*

o   *In the racial unrest of the 1960s, it might have been a black student who stopped to rescue a hood-wearing member of the Ku Klux Klan.*

And today . . . well, if *you* were the one victimized, who would be your Samaritan?

Like the scholar, we have at times been guilty of the same divisive spirit. Such partiality is not compatible with our faith, nor is it a reflection of our Father. Jesus called on his first-century followers to give up their hatred and to love the unlovable; he challenges us to the same quest. And remember, each one of us is unlovable at some point and in some way!

The lesson on prejudice is certainly valuable, but it is only one facet of the parable. More than anything, Jesus taught us how to be good neighbors, how to devote ourselves to doin' good in the hood.

IT'S ABOUT MEETING NEEDS, NOT JUST BEING NEAR

Being a neighbor isn't about spying—Gladys Kravitz-like—on those nearby; it's about watching for those who have needs. When the Samaritan happened upon the brutalized traveler, he didn't inquire as to the man's geographic origin or his Judea zip code. He did what he could to save the man's life. The person's need should determine how we respond as neighbors.

Being a neighbor to someone is also not contingent upon that person's good judgment or common sense. The Samaritan didn't scold the traveler for his carelessness while he bandaged his wounds. Meeting the need was critical—and far more effective than the "What a Stupid Thing to Do" sermon he could have preached. My experience has been that we don't need someone to remind us of our stupidity; we are painfully aware of our mistakes. What we need is someone to help us out of our misery and care for us despite our dumb decisions.

IT'S ABOUT EXCEEDING EXPECTATIONS, NOT OFFERING EXCUSES

The priest and the Levite obviously saw a need, but their excuses trumped their compassion. The priest might have thought, *This could be a trap—if I stop I might become the victim.*

I understand that fear. To be honest, I'm reluctant to stop for a hitchhiker because of the many tragic stories I've heard. It's easy to be critical of the priest, but I have responded similarly. You probably have too.

The Levite might have reasoned, *This will make me ceremonially unclean and prevent me from serving at the temple. Besides, someone else who isn't in such a compromising position will come along to help.* Again, it is easy to rationalize such a response. If we are doing God's work in some unique capacity, we can justify our lack of involvement because surely others will rise to the challenge and meet this need. Besides, my own job may go undone if I stop to meet someone else's need.

The real power behind the Samaritan was his willingness to exceed expectations. He not only empathized with the man, he administered first aid, provided transportation, and paid the bills for his complete recovery. Wow, that was going the second mile and then some! When we go above and beyond what anyone expects or imagines, people notice. Such actions of compassion speak louder than any lesson or sermon ever could!

The year was 1630. The Puritans had loaded the ship *Arabella* and set sail for the New World. Their preacher, John Winthrop, who would later become the governor of Massachusetts, wrote a sermon while en route and preached it mid-Atlantic. (Any preacher worth his salt knows what to do when he has a captive crowd!) The sermon was entitled "A Model of Christian Charity," in which Winthrop outlined the purposes of God for a new England. This excerpt from his sermon tells about his dream to establish a new type of community: "We must be knit together, in this work, as one man. We must entertain each other in brotherly affection. . . . We must delight in each other; make others' conditions our own; rejoice together, mourn together, labor and suffer together, always having before our eyes our commission and community in the work, as members of the same body. So shall we keep the unity of the spirit in the bond of peace."[2]

Now that's what I'd call a great neighborhood! John Winthrop's dream for such a vibrant community in the New World never came to pass as he envisioned it, but his integrity as a man of God and his desire to be a good neighbor never wavered. We would do well to put those principles into practice. People would rather *see* a sermon than sit through one.

IT'S ABOUT SACRIFICE, NOT SATISFACTION

God knows that lasting satisfaction comes from a sacrificial heart. When an Old Testament worshiper presented his offering at the temple, it was to be the best of the flock, without spot or blemish. If he had no flock of his own, he was required to buy a lamb suitable for sacrifice. When Araunah the Jebusite offered to give King David his threshing floor, oxen, and wooden yokes as a sacrifice to God, David graciously declined, saying, "No, I insist on paying you for it. I will not sacrifice to the LORD my God burnt offerings that cost me nothing" (2 Samuel 24:24).

"On June 18, 1940, *The Times* of London published the last letter a young airman wrote to his mother. Pilot Officer V. A. Rosewarne had written: 'The universe is so vast and so ageless that the life of one man can only be justified by the measure of his sacrifice.'"[3]

Here is one of those ironies of life. When it becomes our primary goal to satisfy our own desires at the expense of others' needs, we rarely experience a moment of contentment. On the other hand, when we make sacrifices so that we can invest our lives in others first, we discover a deep sense of satisfaction. Don't hold back. Start looking for specific ways to help someone. Look around—it's not difficult to find hurting people who need you. There is more than one "Bloody Pass" on this rugged journey. Pray as you travel that God will give you Samaritan eyes and a Samaritan heart.

Bloomington, Indiana—my home for the last twenty-seven years—is also home to a uniquely wonderful treatment center called MPRI, Midwest Proton Radiotherapy Institute. Proton therapy is an extremely precise and technical means of delivering radiation to the location of a cancerous tumor or other disease site. This therapy is good news—it attacks the tumor while minimizing the damage to surrounding healthy tissue. Because there are so few proton radiotherapy facilities in the nation, people travel from all over to receive cancer treatment here. For many it is a last-hope stop.

Some time ago our church facilities manager, Phil Thompson, stepped into my office with an idea. You see, not long after MPRI began treating patients, Phil was diagnosed with prostate cancer and was the first prostate patient to receive treatment there. That's only part of the story. Before Phil retired and came to work for us, he had spent most of his career in management for the Indiana University Cyclotron, a nuclear accelerator that creates the beam used in proton radiation. It's amazing how God works so providentially in our lives. Phil helped build the cyclotron, and then it was used to help save his own life!

There is one major challenge for those who come from some distance to MPRI for treatment: housing. The daily radiation treatments can last up to six weeks. It's not a problem for local residents, but those who must travel several hundred miles for this service face quite a logistical nightmare. Phil suggested that our congregation provide housing for these patients while they are in town. It was a great idea, and he was the perfect guy to head up this ministry. It didn't take much encouragement for Phil to accept the challenge.

Since that time, many others in the congregation have joined Phil in the adventure, and the church now has access to five facilities—empty homes or condos—to use for out-of-town patients. Dozens of volunteers enthusiastically give time and energy to serve these people during their stay in Bloomington. When a patient and his family arrive at their home away from home, they are often greeted with fresh flowers, a stocked refrigerator, and some just-baked goodies to make them feel at home. The team doesn't ask about their race, age, religion, or condition—they just open a welcome door.

The adult patients are truly encouraging, and the children who come for treatments move us to tears. Last Christmas two of the teenage boys were comparing their holiday wish lists. Most teens would be asking for electronic gizmos and gadgets, but these boys were different. One was hoping for new teeth; the other, a glass eye. For six weeks such families become a part of our family, and most have chosen to worship with us. The leaving is the hardest part for all concerned—and even after returning home, all have stayed in regular contact.

This ministry, simply called Hoosier Hospitality, has changed more lives at our church than at the clinic. I marvel when I think that God had been preparing Phil throughout his entire life for the ministry of a lifetime. You'd be surprised to know how many "neighbors" Phil has all across the nation. He and the incredible Hoosier Hospitality team are modern-day Good Samaritans. They're doin' good in the hood.

I don't know when I first heard this quote, but it has stuck with me for years: "For me to love the world's no chore; my big problem is the guy next door." The Parable of the Good Samaritan is an inspiring story until it becomes personal. I can profess my love for the world—that's easy; that's not personal. But when it comes to meeting the needs of the cantankerous guy who lives across the street, the druggie who ignores her five unruly kids, the foul-mouthed jerk who hangs out at the corner gas station, the bitter widow who never has a kind word to say . . . well, that's another story—that's personal.

Yes, there are wounded lives on the rocky path all around you. But don't run. Get personal! Someone is just waiting for you to be a neighbor.

1 I had never seen them before (and doubt that I will see them again), but in those few minutes they were neighbors to me. I needed help—desperately—and they came to my rescue!

You've probably known someone who modeled in word and deed what a good neighbor should be. What are some of the most valuable lessons you have gleaned from that person's example? Beginning right now, what can you do to be a better example?

2 Like the scholar, we have at times been guilty of the same divisive spirit. Such partiality is not compatible with our faith, nor is it a reflection of our Father.

What makes one human being prejudiced against another? Do you have any biases? What can you do to break down any prejudicial barriers that you have experienced? In what practical ways can the church be a model of reconciliation?

3 It is not clear whether the scholar was simply repeating what he had been taught or if indeed he understood the powerful truth that loving one's neighbor *is* also a way of loving God.

Why are we so preoccupied with self-indulgence and so quick to dismiss the needs around us when we can make a difference in people's lives? How do you achieve a balance between meeting the needs of others and also meeting the needs in your own home?

4 On the other hand, when we make sacrifices so that we can invest our lives in others first, we discover a deep sense of satisfaction. Don't hold back. Start looking for specific ways to help someone.

Have you ever experienced real satisfaction from helping someone who didn't expect to receive your help? Can you describe the situation? Do you know someone right now who has been wounded on a "Bloody Pass"? What will you do about it?

A community is only a community when the majority of its members are making the transition from "the community for myself" to "myself for the community."
JEAN VANIER

As a boy I loved to climb trees, and our backyard was full of stout old maples that made climbing a real adventure. The most inviting trees, of course, were those whose branches were within reach. It didn't take long to learn that going up was a lot easier than coming down. I remember getting stuck out on a limb—more than once—until I figured out the best way to negotiate a painless descent.

Some people *choose* to get stuck out on a limb. On November 1, 2002, John Quigley climbed fifty feet into the branches of Old Glory, a four-hundred-year-old oak tree near Santa Clarita, California.[1] For the next seventy-one days, the tree became his home; he sequestered himself within its branches to prevent it from being cut down to expand a highway.

Quigley made the choice to stake his claim out on that limb, and it paid off. Eventually a compromise was made. The tree was transplanted.

Have you ever felt like you were stuck out on a limb? Perhaps you took a moral stand and suddenly found yourself stuck out on a limb of principle. Sometimes compromise isn't an option. Or maybe you took a risk to reach out to someone in need and found yourself stuck out on a limb of rejection. Most of us don't like limb sitting. Tree knots don't make comfortable seats; and if you get out too far, it can become rather dangerous!

The Bible tells about a man who was out on a limb because nobody wanted him around. He was a guy that people loved to hate. He worked for the enemy, took the hard-earned money of his countrymen, and lived like a fat cat. Though he was Jewish, he worked as a tax collector for the despised Roman government. No wonder the residents of Jericho avoided Zacchaeus like a bird flu pandemic!

JUST PASSING THROUGH

Near the end of his earthly ministry, Jesus passed through Jericho one last time on his way to Jerusalem. The phrase "passing through" (Luke 19:1) suggests it wasn't his intention to spend much time there, but he did.

It turned out to be quite an eventful day.

While still on the journey, Jesus had taken his disciples aside and warned them concerning what would occur once they reached Jerusalem. Jesus described in detail what would happen to the Son of Man (meaning himself): "He will be handed over to the Romans to be mocked, treated shamefully, and spit upon. They will whip him and kill him, but on the third day he will rise again" (Luke 18:32, 33, *NLT*). For those of us living on this side of the cross, we clearly understand what he was referencing. But for the disciples who still thought in terms of a restored earthly kingdom, this must have created lots of confusion.

And if that weren't enough confusion for the day, the mother of James and John approached Jesus with what she determined was a reasonable request—she being the *only* one who thought it was reasonable. She asked that when Jesus established his new kingdom, one of her sons be given a seat on his right and the other on his left (Matthew 20:20-23). In other words, she was requesting that one be vice president and the other be Speaker of the House. At least she was flexible—it didn't matter which son got which side. Jesus was free to decide that much! Once again, this is evidence they still had the wrong idea concerning Christ's kingdom.

No doubt Jesus was gracious to Mrs. Zebedee, but he informed her and her slightly pretentious sons that they had no clue what they were asking. Indeed, they were clueless about what was yet to take place. However, the rest of the disciples were not clueless about the nature of this request— and they were ticked. They became indignant with the two brothers to the extent that Jesus had to stop and set them all straight. He used the opportunity to teach a lesson about a servant's heart: "Whoever wants to become great among you must be your servant, and whoever wants to be first must be your slave—just as the Son of Man did not come to be served, but to serve, and to give his life as a ransom for many" (Matthew 20:26-28).

I marvel at how little human nature has changed. Every generation has mothers or fathers who think their children deserve the best of everything. You've probably witnessed situations in which coworkers or partners get angry at one another as envy and jealousy seep into their relationships. I have a question for the Lord when I get to Heaven—not a heavy theological one, just something simple: "Lord, did you ever roll your eyes or groan at your disciples' cluelessness?"

That question also causes me to wonder, *Which of our actions would cause Jesus to roll his eyes? Which of our attitudes would prompt him to stop and teach us a lesson about a servant's heart?* It is easy to be critical of the disciples, but we are often just as guilty of unspiritual attitudes.

Finally, Jesus and his companions approached the city gates of Jericho. The crowd was so congested in anticipation of the arrival of the rabbi that it was difficult to move into the city. Before Jesus even made it through the city gates, he was stopped by the cries of a blind man who begged for money on the outskirts of town. Jesus, per the man's request, compassionately restored his sight, and they moved on now with an even larger entourage (Luke 18:35-42). As powerful as the moment was, though, this healing wasn't the big news of the day.

A SMALL MAN WITH BIG POTENTIAL

As Jesus moved down the streets, the crowds gathered to see, hear, or touch him as he passed through. Among the throng of people was a man who wanted to see Jesus perhaps more than anyone else. He was the last person you would expect to find standing there, but the most determined to be there. The problem was, he didn't . . . uh, *stand* very tall. He couldn't see over the others, and they weren't about to let him wriggle through the crowd to stand with the children in front.

Zacchaeus had offended just about everyone in town, but he was determined to see Jesus and would not give up. He finally found a sycamore tree he could climb. This was not the sycamore tree we think of; this is sometimes called a mulberry fig tree, characterized by low, broad, strong branches—good for shade and climbing. Up he went and out on a limb to wait for the only one he truly cared to see. That's when the story really got interesting.

We humans are an odd sort when we experience brushes with fame. I'm convinced that everyone who lined the streets of Jericho that day hoped that Jesus would notice him or her—a smile, a kind word, a nod, or even a touch . . . something that suggested Jesus noticed. We want to be noticed by famous people.

My family had one black-and-white TV when I was growing up. When Saturday night rolled around, that meant it was time to watch *Lawrence Welk*. Not all TV time is the same—an hour of *Lawrence Welk* seemed a lot longer to me than an hour of *Bonanza*! My least favorite member of the bubble-makers was an Irish tenor name Joe Feeney. (In my opinion, no man should be able to hit notes designed only for women's voices.)

One summer a part of the *Lawrence Welk* team came to our county to do a show. It wasn't enough that we had to listen every Saturday night; our family bought tickets for this live show. Only three members of the cast were performing; but of the three, one just happened to be—you guessed it—Joe Feeney. To make matters worse, I ended up on the front row of the school auditorium, so I had to at least *act* like I was interested.

As Joe Feeney began to sing his way toward treble clef range, he started down the stage stairs into the audience. I figured he was going to croon into the eyes of some middle-aged woman and cause palpitations, but no—he walked right over to me and extended his hand. I couldn't believe it; I actually shook hands with a TV star!

The following Saturday night I was parked squarely in front of the old black-and-white, just waiting to hear my favorite Irish tenor sing. Funny, isn't it? Just the touch of someone famous changes our perspective.

Jesus was much more than a celebrity. Those he touched were truly changed. It is no wonder, then, the streets of Jericho were packed with those who dreamed of being noticed by the very Son of God. Yet Luke records just one interaction with the crowd inside the city; Jesus noticed the one everybody else was trying to ignore. Undoubtedly there were many in the crowd who loved Jesus, but Jesus turned his attention to the only one whom no one else loved.

I suspect that Zacchaeus would have preferred to remain inconspicuous— but when you're out on a limb, you make a pretty easy target. With rocks being plentiful along the roadside, he was taking quite a risk. Jesus walked over to the tree, and the crowd grew quiet. They must have been wondering, *Is he looking for shade? Perhaps he wants a fig snack?* Then Jesus uttered the unimaginable words: "Zacchaeus, is that you out on that limb? Come down and take me to your house. I'm going to spend the afternoon with you" (see Luke 19:5).

The crowd was incredulous; they were dumbfounded at this unexpected turn of events. *What's wrong with Jesus—he just healed a blind man and now he can't see? Surely he's been out in the sun too long, and the heat has affected his brain. As soon as Jesus sees who's out on that limb, he'll change his mind.*

But he didn't change his mind; there was nothing wrong with Jesus. Zacchaeus scrambled down the tree and gleefully took off with Jesus and his disciples in tow. The crowd was left stunned in disbelief.

Then the murmuring began: *Maybe this Jesus isn't so smart after all. Were he a prophet or the Messiah, he would know the kind of guy Zacchaeus is, and he would undoubtedly feel just like us.*

But Jesus always saw what the crowd didn't. He looked beyond Zacchaeus's stature, beyond his alliance with the Roman government, and beyond the disdain of the crowd. Jesus recognized a small man with big potential for God.

A grand meal and celebration followed the walk home. The non-elite were invited. (I wouldn't be surprised if Zacchaeus invited a few people who were blind and homeless to join them too.) Picture the scene in his home. Here was the despised tax man hosting Jesus around his own table. Wow! I imagine Zacchaeus thought he'd died and gone to Heaven.

On second thought, that is exactly what happened. After being in the presence of Jesus for that afternoon, Zacchaeus died to his old way of life, and the hope of Heaven filled his heart and soul. He stood up in the presence of the community and promised, "Look, Lord! Here and now I give half of my possessions to the poor, and if I have cheated anybody out of anything, I will pay back four times the amount" (Luke 19:8).

The Jericho of Jesus' day was a very wealthy community. Being a border town it would have had a customs station. It was a place of rich commerce, was located in the most fertile part of Judea, and flaunted the fact that it was home to one of King Herod's palaces.[2]Being a *chief* tax collector, Zacchaeus had others from the IRS (Israelite Robbery Service) working for him and likely received a cut from their take. He would have been wealthy even without cheating, but his confession infers that he had participated in his fair share of unfairly shared taxes.

Regardless of his great wealth, this was a most sacrificial gift by anyone's standards—half of everything to the poor and a quadruple refund for any deceitful business practices. Such recompense was far above anything required by Mosaic law.

And such a promise of restitution could only have come from one who had been changed. The blind man from earlier wasn't the only "blind man" healed that day. Jesus removed the materialistic cataract that clouded the spiritual vision of Zacchaeus; and for the first time in his life, he could truly see.

Zacchaeus's bold statement wasn't an attempt to buy the friendship of Jesus, the praise of the community, or his salvation from God. His pledge was the expression of gratitude to the one who had just restored his life and set him on the road to eternity. And though Zacchaeus couldn't have known it then, in less than a week Jesus would indeed buy his salvation at the cross once and for all.

This is one of the most powerful transformation stories in the New Testament. When it comes to making a difference in the lives of others in the community, we can learn some big lessons from the little man.

LOVE THE UNLOVABLE

Luke 19:5 says, "When Jesus reached the spot, he looked up and said to him, 'Zacchaeus, come down immediately. I must stay at your house today.'" Of the thousands of people in Jericho, any number would have jumped at the chance to host Jesus in their homes; but the Lord chose to love the unlovable. Instead of hobnobbing with the upper crust, he opted to spend time with the down-and-out.

To be honest, I think most of us relate to the crowd more than we relate to Jesus. It's a great story until we transfer the principles to life in the twenty-first century. Stop for a minute and think about the person you dislike most in this world. Maybe he cheated you in a business deal. Maybe she robbed you of a good reputation with her indiscreet gossip. Maybe you were snookered into a financial scam by a "friend" and got left holding the bag—the *empty* bag. As soon as you have an image of that person in mind, proceed to the following questions:

o   *If she walked into a worship service next Sunday and sat down in your row, would you get up and move?*

o   *If he extended his hand, would you refuse to shake it?*

o   *If he smiled, would you return the smile, or just turn away?*

Suppose Jesus walked into the same worship service and asked that person to go to lunch instead of you. Would you question, "Wait a minute, Lord. You don't know him like I do. How can you eat with someone like that?"

While that disgusting image is still fresh in your mind, transfer it to the face of Zacchaeus. Suddenly the crowd's response doesn't seem so unreasonable, does it? We can never afford to forget that while Jesus hates the sinful actions even more than we do, he never stops loving the unlovable.

Jesus knew *everything* about Zacchaeus and loved him despite his sin. It was that extension of kindness and grace that changed this tax collector forever. Extending kindness to the harsh, being gracious to the ungracious, loving the unlovable . . . those are the most difficult challenges we face as Christians. But it is the countercultural attitude— the unexpected response—that impacts a community the most. When you act more like Jesus, it sets you apart; it draws people to Christ in you.

Jesus loved the unlovable Zacchaeus in the presence of the unloving community. Did you catch that? Jesus didn't call Zacchaeus off to the side and whisper his request in his ear. He didn't say something like, "After the crowds are gone and no one notices, I'll quietly slip down to your house for a bite. Leave the gate open; I'll come in through the backyard."

No, he announced it before God and everybody on the street; he left nothing to chance. Jesus was modeling a powerful truth. He wanted the crowd to understand that forgiving what seems unforgivable and loving what seems unlovable isn't easy but it *is* God's expectation. I'm not talking about a wimpy, naive forgiveness by which you become a doormat where others wipe the feet of their soiled living. I'm talking about being very purposeful, loving the unlovable for Christ's sake.

In October 2005 I had the privilege of spending ten days in central India. There I met the most wonderful, dedicated Christians—Christians who put their lives on the line daily for their faith. There was one man, however, whose ministry experience haunts me yet today. His build was slight, and he barely stood as tall as my shoulder . . . an Indian look-alike of Zacchaeus.

I learned that this minister and his wife had once been attacked by Hindu extremists. They forced him to watch as two men raped his wife. The only way out was to renounce his faith. He did not yield, and his good wife pleaded with him to stay strong. Finally, they both were rescued by some people from the community. Had that been me, I would have moved as far away from that community as possible, but not these giants in the faith. They continue to minister in the same area! As a result, one of the extremists has become a believer. Imagine! The former rapist is now a brother; he worships in the same service with the minister and his wife.

That's loving the unlovable in a powerful way. That's going out on a limb.

IGNORE THE NEGATIVE

Luke 19:7 records, "All the people saw this and began to mutter, 'He has gone to be the guest of a "sinner."'" The truth is, it wouldn't have mattered where Jesus ate dinner that day; in anyone's home he would have been "the guest of a 'sinner'"! There will always be negative people who can make life miserable. Being negative does not make one feel better or improve an unpleasant situation.

According to Dr. Elinore Kinarthy, the average person has more than two hundred negative thoughts a day—things like worries, jealousies, and insecurities. Depressed individuals have as many as six hundred. You can't eliminate all the troublesome things that seep into your mind, but you can certainly reduce the number of negative thoughts by replacing them with the positive.[3]

Don't allow the negative attitudes and behaviors of others to cause you to lose heart or give up on the good you are doing. Zacchaeus went out on a limb, ignoring the crowd's negative opinion of him in order to get closer to Jesus. And Jesus went out on a limb, dismissing the pessimistic opinions of the crowd to save the life of Zacchaeus. Be faithful in your work for the Lord, regardless of what those around you may say.

RIGHT OLD WRONGS

Luke 19:8 states, "But Zacchaeus stood up and said to the Lord, 'Look, Lord! Here and now I give half of my possessions to the poor, and if I have cheated anybody out of anything, I will pay back four times the amount.'"

Sometimes it can't happen—sometimes you can't correct a mistake. But when it is possible, right the wrong. A genuinely repentant heart will point others to Jesus Christ.

The month of April has a number of special distinctions. April is National Humor Month, National Stress Awareness Month, and National Garden Month. In addition to the more obvious Administrative Professionals Day and Arbor Day, April includes the lesser-known National Pretzel Day (that adds a real twist!) and National Peanut Butter and Jelly Day. The designation that intrigues me most falls on April 30—National Honesty Day. The day is devoted to promoting honesty in our nation: honest words, intentions, and behavior.

Congress has never issued an official proclamation for National Honesty Day—no surprise there! Nonetheless, it has been observed on April 30 for many years. I like the theme, but why should there be just one day to promote the truth? We don't need pretzels every day, but shouldn't we be honest all the time? If honesty is a virtue we hold in high regard, then it shouldn't be something we find on a calendar; it should be found in our character. I like that about Zacchaeus—he really came clean! The change was seen in his character. No excuses, just promises to make things right. And we don't need a national day of honesty; we need a conviction to be honest every day. No excuses, just promises to make things right.

RESTORE HOPE

In 1983 actress Shirley MacLaine published her spiritual biography, *Out on a Limb*, in which she chronicled her mystic New Age enlightenment that eventually persuaded her to embrace reincarnation. I think she should have entitled the book *Way Out on a Dead Limb*. Tragically, she asked many of the right questions but ended up with false, hopeless answers. Was there no one to restore her hope through Jesus?

The account of Zacchaeus's transformation ends with a statement of hope: "Jesus said to him, 'Today salvation has come to this house, because this man, too, is a son of Abraham. For the Son of Man came to seek and to save what was lost'" (Luke 19:9, 10). Hope prevailed that day:

o   *Zacchaeus's own hope was restored. Jesus forgave his past, affirmed his plan to make a difference in the present, and gave him a future filled with hope.*

o   *Jericho's poor—because of Zacchaeus's generous pledge to share his wealth—possessed hope for better days ahead.*

o   *Jericho's cheated rejoiced in the hope that their losses would be amply restored.*

o   *The whole community was hopeful that they would never again be taken advantage of by Zacchaeus.*

What transformed Zacchaeus from public enemy number one to Jericho's favorite son? It wasn't *what* but *who*. Jesus came to restore lost humanity to God; I can't think of anything more hopeful. That remains the mission of the church today—to seek the seeker, to love the unlovable, and to give hope to the hopeless. That's good news for everyone in town.

DO IT NOW

Jesus was *passing through* Jericho. His destination was Jerusalem and a small grisly hill just outside the city limits. This would be the last time he ever set foot in Jericho. Just think—had Zacchaeus not been so determined to see Jesus, he would have missed the opportunity to see eternity. He had one opportunity and he grabbed it.

Take a good look at your community. What do you see?

o   *hurting people*

o   *homeless people*

o   *helpless people*

o   *hopeless people*

All of them are only one opportunity away from missing out on eternity. Seize the moment—do it now. Follow in the footsteps of Jesus and serve others around you.

In the church we live to give hope. If Jesus can change Zacchaeus, he can change us; he can change anybody. Go out on a limb! Move beyond your backyard and into your community. Love the unlovable, ignore the negative, right the old wrongs, and restore hope. Maybe then our communities will catch a glimpse of the same Jesus that Zacchaeus so desperately wanted to see.

1 Have you ever felt like you were stuck out on a limb? Perhaps you took a moral stand and suddenly found yourself stuck out on a limb of principle. Sometimes compromise isn't an option.

What can you do to build bridges to your community without compromising your principles? Are there times when being out on a limb alone is the right thing to do? Give an example.

2 Of the thousands of people in Jericho, any number would have jumped at the chance to host Jesus in their homes; but the Lord chose to love the unlovable.

Loving the unlovable is not easy, so why do it? What value is there in loving those who may not love us in return? Make a list of ways that you can begin to intentionally love those who are difficult to like.

3 There will always be negative people who can make life miserable. Being negative does not make one feel better or improve an unpleasant situation.

Why do you think so many people respond negatively instead of positively? Do you see the glass half full or half empty? Do you tend to focus on why something *won't* work before focusing on why it *will*? Is being negative compatible with your Christian faith? What can you do to change your negative behavior and attitudes?

4 Sometimes it can't happen—sometimes you can't correct a mistake. But when it is possible, right the wrong.

Righting a wrong takes courage. What other things might it require? How should we respond when we are the offended party? What impact does forgiveness have on another person?

5 Jesus came to restore lost humanity to God; I can't think of anything more hopeful. That remains the mission of the church today—to seek the seeker, to love the unlovable, and to give hope to the hopeless.

What are some practical ways in which the church of the twenty-first century can restore hope to a broken world? Why is it important that we do it now?

It pays to know the enemy—not least because at some time you may have the opportunity to turn him into a friend.
MARGARET THATCHER

Butch. That's the character Tommy Bond played in the Our Gang movie shorts. In fourteen episodes Butch competed with the gangly Alfalfa for sweet Darla's affection and became the consummate silver-screen image of a neighborhood bully. You know the type—big, brash, intimidating . . . and sometimes not so bright.

Bullies have been around since the beginning of time. Nearly every adventure story in God's Word includes one. Here's a small sampling of Bible bullies:

o   *The serpent bullied Eve in the garden with a lie.*

o   *Cain bullied his brother Abel with murderous resentment.*

o   *Goliath bullied David with godless taunts.*

o   *Pharaoh bullied the Israelites with his army on the banks of the Red Sea.*

o   *King Nebuchadnezzar bullied Shadrach, Meshach, and Abednego with a furnace seven times hotter than normal.*

o   *King Darius bullied Daniel with a pride of lions.*

o   *Judas bullied Jesus with a kiss.*

o   *Saul of Tarsus bullied the church with death threats.*

o   *Herod Agrippa I bullied the apostles with arrest—and even killed James.*

Many of the Bible bullies got what they deserved: the serpent was crushed, Cain was marked, Goliath was stoned, Pharaoh's army was washed away, Nebuchadnezzar went insane, Judas committed suicide, and Herod Agrippa I was eaten by worms—yuck!

BULLYING GOD

At one time or another, practically everyone has faced off against a backyard tyrant. And bullies don't disappear after childhood. They aren't limited to school playgrounds or neighborhood turf wars; they can also show up in factories, fraternities, and even families. Jesus himself had to deal with bullies—not just once, but several times throughout his three-year ministry. The climax came shortly before the cross. In the most stressful hours of his life, Jesus was being bullied by people who should have reached out to him.

Let's set the stage: From the moment Jesus arose from the watery grave of his Jordan River baptism, he had to deal with difficult and obnoxious people—scribes, teachers of the law, and Pharisees. They were the bullies of the Judean badlands. And yet they didn't fit the stereotypical image of a bully.

These bad guys came from the upper crust of society and from what would have been known as the Religious Right of their day. Actually, they feared Jesus. Their misguided perspective convinced them that they had everything to lose and nothing to gain from Jesus' intrusion into Jewish society. Just the opposite was true. These religious oppressors were about to lose everything they had gained because they bullied the very Son of God.

Arrogantly, these bullies appeared in public places as society's cream of the crop, but their true characters were forged in the places where one expects to find bullies—dark corners, back alleys, and deep shadows.

In the Sermon on the Mount, Jesus communicated some tough standards that can help us deal with bullies. Jesus always practiced what he preached. But his directives cut across the grain of human nature:

o *Turn the other cheek.*

o *Go the second mile.*

o *Give to the one who asks.*

o *Don't do good deeds to be seen by others.*

o *Don't be hypocritical when you pray.*

o *Don't trust in your wealth.*

o *Don't worry about tomorrow.*

Invigorating words to hear—tough words to practice. We often like to quote the familiar verbal gems, but nestled among these countercultural paradigms is one imperative we seldom reference. In truth, we wish it weren't even part of the text. Check out these uncomfortable words: "But I tell you who hear me: Love your enemies, do good to those who hate you, bless those who curse you, pray for those who mistreat you" (Luke 6:27, 28).

Perhaps Jesus didn't really mean what he said. Maybe his tongue got tangled on this one, and the disciples simply got confused—again! Or perhaps something was lost in the translation from the Aramaic to the English. There has to be some other explanation, right? Sorry. If this were the only text of its kind, we *might* look for some excuse to try and pick it apart, but it does not stand alone. If you think these words of Jesus from the Sermon on the Mount are tough, wait until you read how a former bully penned the same idea in Romans 12:14-21:

> Bless those who persecute you; bless and do not curse. Rejoice with those who rejoice; mourn with those who mourn. Live in harmony with one another. Do not be proud, but be willing to associate with people of low position. Do not be conceited.
>
> Do not repay anyone evil for evil. Be careful to do what is right in the eyes of everybody. If it is possible, as far as it depends on you, live at peace with everyone. Do not take revenge, my friends, but leave room for God's wrath, for it is written: "It is mine to avenge; I will repay," says the Lord. On the contrary:
>
> "If your enemy is hungry, feed him; if he is thirsty, give him something to drink. In doing this, you will heap burning coals on his head."
>
> Do not be overcome by evil, but overcome evil with good.

Considering Jesus' words in the Sermon on the Mount and Paul's words in his letter to the church at Rome, we cannot escape this uncomfortable lesson. We need to stop looking for an alternate way to explain this principle and start looking for an acceptable way to apply it in dealing with our backyard bullies!

The religious aristocracy seemed to enjoy bullying Jesus, the Galilean preacher. Always looking for a way to dismiss him, they questioned his parentage, his ethics, his Hebrew loyalty, his association with the lower class, his choice of disciples, and most of all his faith. With every passing month, the intensity of their verbal attacks grew. However, their carefully chosen words and semantic gymnastics could not squelch the popularity of this renegade rabbi. Finally it was determined that a death sentence was the only viable solution. As any gang of bullies would do, they schemed, plotted, and conspired to arrest Jesus. He knew the day would come when his love-your-enemies code of conduct would be tested to the max.

A GODLY RESPONSE

In the waning hours of his ministry, Jesus gathered with his disciples one final time in an upper room to share a last meal and mark the Feast of Unleavened Bread. Having sung a song of praise, they crossed the Kidron Valley and entered the beautiful garden on the crest of the Mount of Olives.

Jesus knew what was about to happen, but the disciples were still clueless. As they walked toward the garden, Jesus gave them a veiled warning: "When I sent you out to minister, I told you not to take any provisions but to make it a journey of faith. And all your needs were supplied, right? But now, if you have money, hang on to it. If you don't have a sword, sell your coat and buy one" (see Luke 22:35, 36). Then Jesus quoted from Isaiah 53 about being "numbered with the transgressors," suggesting that the disciples' relationship with him would soon implicate them as well. This wasn't about hoarding goods for the near future; it was about fighting for their very existence.

Neither was this a call to arms, but a prophetic way of communicating that their lives were at stake. The disciples just couldn't seem to grasp the picture yet. Jesus' reference to a sword caused them to take immediate inventory of their weapons. A moment later they proudly produced two swords. Jesus responded, "That is enough" (Luke 22:38). The context of the passage and the character of Christ clearly suggest that Jesus was not concerned that his band of eleven possessed enough swords to physically defend themselves. Rather, it may have been an expression of exasperation—"That is enough of this nonsense."[1] Several versions of the Bible translate these words from verse 38 as, "Enough of that." Certainly the disciples didn't yet understand the kind of kingdom Jesus had come to establish.

Following an agonizing time of prayer, Jesus and the disciples headed out of the garden. Judas—along with a detachment of soldiers and an entourage of accomplices—was just arriving to arrest the Lord.

This is where the story's intensity picks up.

The high priest, Pharisees, and religious leaders wanted Jesus dead. No detail had been overlooked. The turncoat Judas had been hired to identify Jesus in the dead of night when the masses of people who loved the Savior were asleep. A whole band of soldiers had been procured. A mock trial was planned down to the last witness. Intent on protecting their turf, these Jewish leaders were not about to soil their hands with a messy arrest, so they sent others to do their dirty work. It is likely that many of these henchmen had not seen Jesus up close, if they had seen him at all. Judas's kiss was necessary to identify Jesus in the darkness, lest they grab the wrong man and Jesus escape into the shadows.

The high priest was at the pinnacle of Jewish society—as powerful and wealthy as anyone. On this dreadful occasion the high priest sent his servant as a personal representative of himself and his office. The trusted servant, named Malchus (John 18:10), undoubtedly was at the forefront of this armed band, leading with all the clout of Annas and Caiaphas. This man was not an innocent bystander who simply got caught in the chaos. Malchus was eager to protect the rule and authority of his master.

When the two parties met, Judas stepped forward to greet the giver of life with the kiss of death. Matthew and Mark both indicate with their word choice that Judas kissed him profusely.[2] Perhaps he was trying to salve a guilty conscience. The betrayer then stepped away so those in authority could seize Jesus. Finally, the disciples woke up to the realization of what was happening. They cried out, "Lord, should we strike with our swords?" (Luke 22:49). Without waiting for an answer, Peter grabbed one of the two cutlasses and lunged toward the closest target at hand—Malchus. Peter was hardly intent on disfiguring the assailant; he was ready to decapitate him. Peter swung. Malchus ducked. An ear fell.

First blood had been drawn by the rebels, and the battle-hardened soldiers were poised to retaliate. One could hear the rising metallic sound of what seemed to be hundreds of swords being unsheathed. Jesus' enemies stood before him, intent on seeing him crucified. Heaven breathlessly watched. Twelve legions of armed angels (that is, seventy-two thousand) hovered on the brink of eternity waiting for the call to battle (Matthew 26:53).

With a word Jesus had calmed raging seas; at that moment he could just as easily have destroyed his raging enemies with a word. Instead, he extended his hand to the bleeding bully and instantly restored his ear. We don't know whether he reached down in the dirt and picked up the cartilage, placing it in its rightful spot on the side of his head, or just cupped his hand around the ear hole and gave Malchus a new look. How he accomplished the miracle doesn't really matter; the fact that he miraculously healed the bully's ear changed everything. In that moment Jesus demonstrated uncommon mercy—he put into practice the toughest of his own commands.

Little things are often overlooked. It was just an ear. Luke alone bothers to record this miracle that took place in the midst of murderers. Ironic, isn't it? This was the last miracle before Jesus' death; and it was bestowed, like a medal of valor, upon his *enemy*. Incredibly, the name Malchus means "king."[3] There in the darkness of an olive grove, two "kings" met—one motivated by the power of greed, the other motivated by the power of grace.

Mel Gibson's interpretation of this encounter in *The Passion of the Christ* is riveting. The Gospel accounts leave us to wonder what happened to Malchus after this experience. Did he exit the garden with the troops, or stay there to contemplate the goodness of God? Did a physical touch change his spiritual outlook? How often did he reach up to touch his ear and think of the compassionate Christ? Did the apostle John, writing much later than the others, specifically mention the name Malchus because the early church would have recognized him as a faithful convert?

Such speculations will likely be overlooked by most; what cannot be ignored, however, is the inspiring response of Jesus toward these bullies in the night. How he handled such difficult people challenges us to find a way to do the same.

HOW CAN I HANDLE OBNOXIOUS, DIFFICULT PEOPLE?

I was in fourth or fifth grade and had a brand-new winter coat. That in itself was pretty exciting; new clothes or new shoes didn't come along very often. On the first day I wore the coat to school, the weather was one of those in-between days: not quite freezing but almost. The puddles on the playground were slushy, hovering between ice and water. When I went out for morning recess, Danny Patmore was waiting for me. To this day I don't know why, but he was. Maybe he was in an ornery mood from a bad grade, maybe he thought I was no threat since I was smaller than he was, or maybe my new coat was just too great a temptation.

As I walked past Danny, he stepped forward, stuck his foot into my path, and then pushed me into a huge slush puddle. My new coat was soaked, and I was ticked. He stood there and didn't say a word, but he had a very satisfied smile on his face. That put me over the edge. I got up (though not as heroically as I would have liked, since my water-soaked coat now weighed twice what it had before), reared back, and socked him in the jaw. Hey, I'd seen it work for John Wayne in the old West, so why not on the old playground? Danny never said a word. His eyes got red, and he lost that smug smile; then he turned and walked off. It was the first and last time I ever punched anyone in the jaw.

Looking back on that experience now, it certainly wasn't the best way to handle the situation. Sure, Danny had acted like a jerk, but that was no way for me to react. It definitely wasn't a Christian reflection of loving your neighbor as yourself, doing good to those who mistreat you, or repaying evil with good. If one of my teachers had seen me, I would have been in deep trouble. (And I sure wished John Wayne had mentioned in some movie how much your fist hurts after doing that.)

Bullies aren't limited to the playground; they are everywhere. Some are easy to spot—loud, forceful, pushy, gruff, intimidating, threatening, and menacing. You know the type.

Others are not so obvious and show up in the most surprising places.

BULLIES IN THE CHURCH

Those who bullied Jesus were supposed to be the good guys—the ones you'd expect to be wearing the white hats and riding white horses. It's hard when those who profess to be close to God are so obnoxious and difficult. The very people who should have been the most supportive and welcoming ended up being the greatest roadblocks for Jesus.

When I arrived early on the first night of a revival I was to preach, only three or four members of the congregation were in the building. One rather crotchety older man made a beeline for me, recognizing me as the guest speaker. He pointed to the old Seth Thomas on the wall and said, "See that clock—I expect you to use it!" Then without so much as a handshake or a "glad you're here," he turned and walked away.

I'd met the church bully. I didn't have to be a cardiologist to know his heart wasn't in the right place. I was tempted to preach for a couple of hours that first night just to make him squirm, but I decided that wouldn't be fair to everyone else.

The world has more than its share of insufferable people, but the church should be free of such individuals.

All people are certainly welcome in the church, but as they learn to imitate Christ, obnoxious behavior must go. Such actions and attitudes would hardly be compatible with those who are sincere in following Jesus.

BULLIES IN THE OFFICE

Working with certain coworkers or for some bosses can be a pain. A difficult colleague or obnoxious supervisor can make going to work sheer drudgery. Rainy days and Mondays can't compare to the discouragement created by the office bully. He can take the joy right out of working nine to five.

When you encounter such an individual, try to remember to ask yourself why this person treats others the way he does. Does he just have a need to be in charge or always be right? Does he treat others this way in an attempt to elevate himself? Do the roots of his behavior stem from an unhappy life at home? Knowing what drives him to act in a negative manner may help you know how best to respond.

BULLIES IN THE HOME

At times a spouse can act in the most obnoxious manner. We all mess up occasionally—saying and doing things to make life difficult for our spouses—but some spouses are simply bullies all the time.

I like this modern-day fairy tale:

> Once upon a time, a beautiful, independent, and confident princess happened upon a frog in a pond. The frog said to the princess, "I was once a handsome prince until an evil witch put a spell on me. One kiss from you, and I will turn back into that handsome prince. Then we can marry, move into the castle with my mother, and you can prepare my meals, wash my clothes, clean the palace, bear my children, and forever feel happy doing so."
>
> That night, while the princess dined on frog legs, she kept laughing and saying, "I don't think so . . . I don't think so!"

If a good punch in the jaw isn't the best answer, then how *should* we handle obnoxious, difficult people?

SEEK TO UNDERSTAND

Some individuals would never use the term *bully* to describe themselves. The notorious gangster Al Capone, who terrorized Chicago during the Depression, regarded himself quite differently. He said, "I have spent the best years of my life giving people the lighter pleasures, helping them have a good time, and all I get is abuse, the existence of a hunted man."[4] The feds regarded Capone as public enemy number one, but Al saw himself as an unappreciated and misunderstood public *benefactor*. That's a pretty extreme example, but it does give us a glimpse into human nature.

Few people are naturally bullies; most are hurting, scared, or discouraged. You just might be a convenient target when they are ready to unload with both barrels. Or you could represent someone who seems to have it all together, and they resent you for it. By reaching out to them with understanding, you might win a friend when you would otherwise make an enemy.

As I think back to that day on the playground . . . Danny Patmore was probably frustrated and discouraged about something. And I may have been an easy release for his frustration. If I had been a little older and wiser, I might have been more understanding. And had I understood better, I would have reacted better . . . possibly. Understanding *is* the first step in getting along with difficult people.

APOLOGIZE WHEN WRONG

When someone acts obnoxiously toward you, find out whether you have done something to offend—intentionally or unintentionally. If you have offended the person, apologize. Amazingly, a heartfelt apology can heal some misunderstandings. Jesus instructed his disciples about approaching someone who had acted in an offensive manner: "If a fellow believer hurts you, go and tell him—work it out between the two of you. If he listens, you've made a friend" (Matthew 18:15, *The Message*).

The converse of that divine principle must also be true. When you are the one who is guilty of the offense, listen to the complaint, work it out, and build a friendship on forgiveness.

DON'T RETALIATE

Only the Lord can exact fair and just vengeance. We never *even* the score—when we try we only cause the hostility to escalate. Jesus never retaliated, though he certainly had the right to. If he didn't do so, we have no justification for behaving that way.

The apostle Paul has some great and easy to understand advice for us: "Do not repay anyone evil for evil. Be careful to do what is right in the eyes of everybody. If it is possible, as far as it depends on you, live at peace with everyone. Do not take revenge, my friends, but leave room for God's wrath, for it is written: 'It is mine to avenge; I will repay,' says the Lord" (Romans 12:17-19).

Don't compromise your character or integrity. When you lower yourself to the offender's style of behavior, you are no better than he is. Rise above such actions—be known for always doing what is right.

HOW CAN I AVOID BECOMING AN OBNOXIOUS, DIFFICULT PERSON?

Of the two main questions explored in this chapter, this is by far the more important and uncomfortable one to consider.

BE SELF-CONTROLLED

Jesus was. If you want to be known for your self-control, don't sock people in the jaw. Proverbs 25:28 says, "Like a city whose walls are broken down is a man who lacks self-control." Behave the same day in and day out, regardless of where you are or whom you are with. Being consistent will help you avoid becoming a difficult person.

BE GENUINELY CONCERNED FOR OTHERS

Notice what Paul wrote in Romans 12:15. He charged us to "rejoice with those who rejoice; mourn with those who mourn." In other words, be genuinely concerned for others in your life circle. When something good happens to a social acquaintance, don't be inwardly resentful that it didn't happen to you. When a colleague goes through a tough time, don't offer plastic sympathy while inwardly feeling a bit smug. Go out of your way to demonstrate godly concern. A genuinely caring person is seldom mistaken for being obnoxious.

BE HARMONIOUS

Isn't that what Paul instructed? "As far as it depends on you, live at peace with everyone." Find a way to get along with others. Look for the best, not the worst. Encourage the positive and avoid criticism. To disparage another's faults only accentuates our own. When we point out the speck in a neighbor's eye, the rest of the neighborhood is quick to point out the log hanging out of ours.

Find common ground. The cross is a good place to start; the ground is always equal there.

BE HUMBLE

Be genuinely humble, but don't flaunt it before others. Being proud of your humility defeats the purpose! Perhaps you've heard about the man who was presented with a medal for being the most humble man in church; but when he *wore* the medal the following Sunday, the church had to take it back.

An arrogant or prideful attitude never points to Christ. Learn to treat everyone alike, regardless of their backgrounds, education, social position, or financial standing. No one is better than another. Genuine humility is never confused with an obnoxious, difficult spirit.

In Dale Carnegie's classic book, *How to Win Friends and Influence People*, he deals with the struggle to avoid being a difficult and obnoxious person. The section entitled "Six Ways to Make People Like You" contains six principles that are worth imitating. They are as follows:

o   *Become genuinely interested in other people.*

o   *Smile.*

o   *Remember that a person's name is to that person the sweetest and most important sound in any language.*

o   *Be a good listener. Encourage others to talk about themselves.*

o   *Talk in terms of the other person's interests.*

o   *Make the other person feel important—and do it sincerely.*[5]

The naval cruiser USS *Vincennes* patrolled the waters of the Persian Gulf in July 1988. When the ship's captain mistakenly concluded that the vessel was under attack, he ordered a single missile fired. The missile found its target, an Iranian airliner, and all 290 passengers died. It was a grievous error. When President Reagan decided to compensate the victims' families, public opinion turned against him. Polls revealed that most Americans opposed his actions. The cruel treatment of Americans held hostage by some Iranian bullies was still fresh in the minds of many. In response to one reporter's comment that such a payment would send the wrong message and set a bad precedent, the president wisely answered, "I don't ever find compassion a bad precedent."[6]

Bullies have been around for a long time, and they aren't going away anytime soon. They are never pleasant nor easy to handle. When you've had your fill of their brash and intimidating bravado and you rear back to sock them in the jaw . . . stop! Think of Malchus's ear and Jesus' miracle, and remember that compassion is never a bad precedent.

1 At one time or another, practically everyone has faced off against a backyard tyrant. And bullies don't disappear after childhood. They aren't limited to school playgrounds or neighborhood turf wars; they can also show up in factories, fraternities, and even families.

What is your most memorable encounter with a bully? If you had the opportunity to do it over again, would you change your response? How? Have you found that being an adult has lessened, or increased, the number of bullies you face?

2 What cannot be ignored, however, is the inspiring response of Jesus toward these bullies in the night. How he handled such difficult people challenges us to find a way to do the same. How can I handle obnoxious, difficult people?

What can you do to better understand the actions of the obnoxious people in your life? Why should you apologize if you are not in the wrong? If retaliating will make you feel better, why shouldn't you try to even the score a little? When you respond to a bully *like* a bully, what does that do to your character?

3 Bullies aren't limited to the playground; they are everywhere. Some are easy to spot—loud, forceful, pushy, gruff, intimidating, threatening, and menacing. You know the type. Others are not so obvious and show up in the most surprising places.

How could anyone be a bully in church? What do you do when you find one just down the row from you? What can you do to overcome the attitude of a coworker who bullies you on the job? Have you ever bullied your spouse or been bullied by a spouse? What was the result? What can you do to get past that heartbreak?

4 How can I avoid becoming an obnoxious, difficult person? Of the two main questions explored in this chapter, this is by far the more important and uncomfortable one to consider.

Have you ever been a bully yourself? Explain how the following principles will keep you from becoming a bully to one degree or another: Be self-controlled. Be genuinely concerned for others. Be harmonious. Be humble.

The world is before you, and you need not take it or leave it as it was when you came in.
JAMES BALDWIN

You can see them in many of the backyards of American neighborhoods or subdivisions. Tall and sometimes decorative, they are aptly named privacy fences. Well-meaning people erect these border guards for several reasons:

o   *to keep pets and kids inside the yard*

o   *to cut down on the information available for the neighborhood gossip guild*

o   *to keep unwanted people off the property*

Long before privacy fences became so popular, people planted shrubbery along property lines to accomplish the same purpose. It took longer, naturally, but the hedge eventually shut out the world beyond the backyard. I certainly understand the need for fencing (we had a dog for more than fifteen years), but there is something less than welcoming about a privacy fence or impenetrable hedge.

I think back to the neighborhood where I grew up . . . No one had a privacy border. Our yards all mingled together—that's where we played. It is difficult for me to imagine growing up in a neighborhood where each home is fenced in.

Over sixty years ago Allied troops landed on the beaches of Normandy, France, in the D-Day invasion of Europe. Once past the beachhead, the troops encountered intense resistance in the French countryside. The main obstacle before them was not a better-equipped or better-trained enemy, but a unique terrain created by generations of farmers. The countryside was full of hedgerows, fields ringed with high earthen mounds covered with dense foliage. These naturally grown hedgerows made victory costly and nearly impossible.

In a very real sense, the church has struggled with "hedgerows" and "privacy fences" through the centuries. Each generation has its own hedges. The first-century believers built a privacy fence around the Jewish church to keep out the Gentiles. That certainly wasn't God's plan, so he took action. One afternoon while the apostle Peter prayed, he had what must have seemed like a nightmare about eating wild hogs, dirty birds, and bottom-feeder fish. It was God's special-delivery vision to tear down the fence of prejudice. Shortly after Peter "awoke" (with an upset stomach?), Cornelius became the first baptized Gentile member of the church (Acts 10). It required a supernatural vision and a bit of divine persuasion, but the church finally got beyond the no-Gentile hedgerow.

In the Middle Ages the Crusaders tried to build a privacy fence around the Holy Land, as if the true kingdom of Heaven could exist only in the actual dust where the feet of Jesus had walked. Battles were fought and blood was shed for control of the land that contained the empty tomb of Jesus. Thankfully, those conflicts are but a distant echo in the hedgerows of history.

Through the years other conflicts have arisen—hedges have been built around things like worship styles, strong opinions, divisive prejudice, and political issues. Such hedges have a negative impact. They only isolate the church from her divine mission of serving others for Christ's sake.

What hedgerows encompass the congregation where you worship?

TEARING DOWN FENCES

The church doesn't have the luxury of building privacy fences. The world grows smaller every minute. Sure, it's still nearly twenty-five thousand miles in circumference, but it definitely *feels* smaller. Pick up the phone and call tech support for your computer . . . and you might want to brush up on your Hindi. More than likely you will speak with a technician halfway around the globe in India or Pakistan. Some McDonald's restaurants are now outsourcing their drive-through orders. When you place an order, you may actually be talking to an employee a few states away, who then relays your order to the person at the window. That seems like a lot of fuss for a burger and fries, but apparently it provides more efficient service.[1]

Truly the earth is shrinking. In 1873 Jules Verne wrote his classic novel, *Around the World in Eighty Days,* but today the airline industry can transport you to any major city in a matter of hours. Log on with your BlackBerry or iPhone, and you have instant connectivity with what is happening in the world at any given moment. I never dreamed that the day would come when a sermon I preached in Bloomington, Indiana, could be podcast for use by a church member on business travel in Singapore. (Actually, I never dreamed that anyone would *want* to download one of my sermons, even if the technology developed!)

Despite today's ease of traveling to and communicating with places around the world, I feel most comfortable at home. If you are like me, home is the refuge where you feel safe and content. Sometimes I just want the world to slow down so I can catch my breath. I long to set up the hammock and relax in my own backyard.

Unfortunately, the world continues to spin at one thousand miles per hour, and since nearly 6,400 people die every hour, there is no time to waste. We cannot stay in our own backyards and build hedges to make us feel secure. We must get beyond the hedge if we are to fulfill God's plan for our lives.

The apostle Paul made tents, but he did not build fences. He was globally minded. He didn't think in terms of his *own* backyard; he thought in terms of God's *big* backyard. Paul sensed God's leading and knew his purpose in life was beyond the hedge. Leaving behind what was familiar, Paul jumped over the fence—beyond the comfort of his own backyard—and made history. Let's look in on the life of Paul.

Paul, his new partner Silas, and his son in the faith Timothy headed out from their own backyard in Antioch to revisit and strengthen the Gentile churches established on Paul's previous journey. By the time they arrived in Troas (a city located about ten miles from the ancient city of Troy), Paul had had a unique dream. It wasn't about a Trojan horse, although it *did* contain a surprise for Paul. The divine vision consisted of a Macedonian man pleading, "Come over to Macedonia and help us" (Acts 16:9). Paul took the message to heart, and the team sailed to Greek and Macedonian territory. This was the first time the gospel was preached on the European continent.

While in Europe, Paul and his companions established churches in Philippi, Thessalonica, and Berea—but not without difficulty. The beyond-the-hedge gang was opposed, jailed, ridiculed, and chased out of every town. When the mob caught up with them in Berea, the believers hustled Paul to Athens where he was to remain incognito until Silas and Timothy could catch up with him.

Paul, however, was never able to keep a low profile. As he waited for the rest of the team to arrive, he meandered through the streets of Athens, getting a feel for the people and the culture of the place. Though by the time of Paul's visit Athens had lost some of her glory, she was still a city known as a center of art and education. Many of the philosophers of the day found their home in Athens and spent their time in the marketplaces, discussing the most current ideas and thoughts.[2] Paul was in his element. He seized the moment—and the Areopagus stage—to proclaim the resurrection truth he was so willing to die for.

Paul made sure that what had happened in Jerusalem didn't stay in Jerusalem. How Paul interacted with those Europeans who lived beyond his backyard serves as a great example for us. What is God leading you to do in his big backyard? As you prepare to move beyond your backyard, consider Paul's hedge-hopping style.

BE READY WITH A PLAN

Paul began his life in Tarsus, a large city just off the northeast corner of the Mediterranean Sea. At one time Tarsus had a population of half a million, was a major communication hub, and was the place where Western and Eastern cultures met. The city had been greatly influenced by Greek culture, though it was located at the opposite end of the Mediterranean. A Roman city of immense wealth, Tarsus provided Paul with his natural-born citizenship in the empire.[3]

Paul also grew up as a strict Jewish Pharisee, learning under the teaching of one of the more famous Jewish rabbis, Gamaliel. Paul could not have known it growing up, but his incredible heritage prepared him for the ministry of a lifetime. His knowledge of Greek culture, his Roman citizenship, and his ardent faith made him the obvious choice to take the gospel to the world beyond the backyard of Jerusalem. Paul was a seasoned adult before all the pieces came together for him, but God had a plan that had started back when Paul was a child playing on the riverbank in Tarsus.

God has a plan for your life too. You may not have discovered it at this point, but it's there. The timing may not be right yet, your training may not be complete, all the pieces may not quite be in place . . . but God has a plan. When I was a child, I wanted to be an airline pilot or a doctor—anything but a preacher!—but God had a slightly different plan. While I played in my backyard, little did I know what I would someday be doing in God's backyard.

While it's true that God has a plan for each of our lives, he never wants us to sit on our hands just waiting for him to lead. Paul's strategy was impressive. He, with Silas and Timothy, headed out to visit the churches that he had planted on his first trip. His plan was to then go beyond, God willing, into new territory. Paul had it all mapped out. He preached in what was Galatia and Phrygia with the intention of going north into Bithynia, but the Lord prevented him from going there. Going north was not God's plan, but God did use Paul's plan to get them to Troas. From Troas it was a short cruise to Macedonia.

Paul was a scholar, a man of impeccable Hebrew heritage, and one whose zeal for the living God consumed him. Because he genuinely loved God, he also loved the things that God loved. The best barometer of one's love for God is the answer to this question: How much do I love what and who God loves? Can we honestly claim to genuinely love God when we care more about ourselves than about those who don't know him yet? What are you doing to love God by loving others? Do you have any plans?

Several summers ago our family joined other Sherwood Oaks members for family camp in Mexico. It was a wonderful experience! For our daughters, then ages fourteen and twelve, it marked their first trip south of the border. We slept in a tent, took bucket showers, used outdoor privies, and built five houses for families living in the Tijuana area. It changed our lives—especially our daughters'. Growing up in the church had been a very positive experience for them, but stepping beyond their backyard and building a house for a family who was worlds apart taught Emily and Rebekah more about loving God than scores of Dad's sermons alone could have done.

The camp is an annual ministry of our congregation, and our girls have returned to Mexico more than once to demonstrate their love for God by using hammers and saws. Undoubtedly, their lives are richer today because they got beyond the hedge of our American culture.

In a time when illegal immigration fuels heated discussions throughout our country and our national leaders argue about what kind of fence to build along our southern border, it's good to get beyond the hedge and build a house of love. Look for ways to love God by loving what and who he loves. Then make a plan!

BE PREPARED FOR INTERRUPTIONS

Our best-laid plans may be interrupted by God. When Paul and his team left Antioch, they had every intention of going north; but that plan was interrupted by a divine vision. God sent them in the opposite direction—southwest.

Only God knows what would have happened had they ignored the vision and gone north, but history records the incredible difference Paul's obedience to that interruption made: the church was planted in the cities of Philippi, Thessalonica, Berea, Athens, and more.

The natural question to ask is, "If God may interrupt us, why should we make a plan?" Simple. God often works with and through our plans. Had Paul and Silas not launched out from Antioch, they would not have been in the right place at the right time to enter Europe.

Short-term mission trips are still the subject of much debate. From a missionary's perspective, I can clearly understand how some visits interrupt the actual work of the mission and perhaps impede its operation. However, from a pastoral perspective, I have seen how lives are dramatically changed when people get beyond the hedges of their lives and do something risky and sacrificial for the good of the kingdom.

In any given year some two hundred people from Sherwood Oaks interrupt their schedules to spend time in a dozen countries on at least five different continents—North America, South America, Asia, Europe, and Africa. These volunteers do all sorts of work:

o   *assist in medical hospitals, eye clinics, and first-aid distribution sites*

o   *mix concrete, pound nails, and shingle roofs*

o   *teach children, sing songs, and help kids create VBS crafts*

o   *make beds, clean bathrooms, cook, wash dishes, and complete much-needed maintenance tasks*

o   *teach leaders, lead seminars, and encourage other believers*

o   *distribute food, clothing, and special Christmas gifts*

o   *play soccer, hug children, tie shoes, laugh, and make friendships that will last beyond a lifetime*

o   *grow spiritually, sacrifice, pray, and make a positive difference in a needy world*

In short, these people are a blessing and are blessed in their service—and fall in love with the Lord all over again. These adventures are not unique to our congregation in Bloomington. Thousands of churches send out short-term workers all over the world. For most it is a welcome interruption that changes their lives forever.

But if you can't go on a short-term mission trip, don't worry. You are not a second-class citizen in the kingdom of God. Getting out of your backyard may not take you out of the mainland, but it can take you to Main Street, U.S.A. The world you are to impact may not be a thousand miles away but just beyond the hedge and down the road. Become a friend to a lonely resident in your local senior care center, be a Big Brother or Big Sister, or teach a class on a life skill or hobby you enjoy.

Of course, even "down the road" may be impossible for some people. But physical restrictions or life stages that limit one's mobility don't have to keep you barricaded behind the hedge. I know people who from their wheelchairs have "gone" farther with their prayers, words of praise, encouraging notes, and financial gifts than most of us who know no limitations.

The point is to be willing to allow your daily life to be interrupted in order to "go" somehow.

BE PASSIONATE FOR THE TRUTH

I love Paul's passion for the truth. I also love his passion for people. While he was waiting for Silas and Timothy to arrive, he wasn't cooling his heels in the whirlpool down at the Athenian Hyatt or sipping an espresso with double latte at the Areopagus Starbucks. Instead, Paul roamed the streets and marketplaces, absorbing all he could about the people and culture of Athens. In his quest he discovered that truth was lacking. Luke records: "While Paul was waiting for them in Athens, he was greatly distressed to see that the city was full of idols" (Acts 17:16).

The word "distressed" here carries the idea of being infuriated. Paul was flat-out angry at what he saw. Idols and altars were everywhere—and they covered every conceivable god from Apollo to Zeus. In the face of such rampant idolatry, Paul was desperate for these people to know the truth.

"Then they took him and brought him to a meeting of the Areopagus, where they said to him, 'May we know what this new teaching is that you are presenting? You are bringing some strange ideas to our ears, and we want to know what they mean'" (vv. 19, 20).

These verses sound like they could have been lifted from a postmodern conversation in any café equipped with Wi-Fi. The people of Athens were inquirers, seekers, and philosophers. They embraced the new and unusual. They listened to and carefully weighed the thoughts and words of the speaker. The setting isn't all that different from a twenty-first century university town. People are still seeking the truth.

Truth is important. I like what Franklin P. Jones wrote: "Always tell the truth. You may make a hole in one when you're alone on the golf course someday."4 The political correctness of our current culture seeks to soften, distort, or even obscure the truth; but truth cannot be diminished by our attempts to veil it. We can ignore it, reject it, dismiss it, argue against it, and try to bury it; but like the Energizer Bunny, truth keeps going and going and . . .

Paul suffered greatly because he was passionate about the truth. His uncompromising commitment to what he knew to be true resulted in social rejection, public humiliation, bodily punishment, immobilizing imprisonment, and ultimately, death.

Taking a stand for God's truth will not always be easy. At times you will be viewed as narrow-minded, extreme, intolerant, arrogant, and mean spirited.

By its very nature, truth can antagonize, ostracize, and polarize. The same words of Jesus that appealed to the crowds antagonized the Pharisees. But God's truth can just as easily liberate a captive mind, heal a broken heart, or ease a fearful soul. Jesus reminded those who believed in him, "You will know the truth, and the truth will set you free" (John 8:32).

President Abraham Lincoln understood the awesome power of truth. Perhaps no president in our history experienced its divisive nature more. Lincoln said, "The shepherd drives the wolf from the sheep's throat, for which the sheep thanks the shepherd as his liberator, while the wolf denounces him for the same act as the destroyer of liberty."[5] Truth is liberating and polarizing at the same time. Lincoln also said, "I am not bound to win, but I am bound to be true. I am not bound to succeed, but I am bound to live by the light that I have. I must stand with anybody that stands right and stand with him while he is right, and part with him when he goes wrong."[6] Convicted by the constitutional truth that "all men are created equal," Lincoln abolished slavery—only to be "abolished" himself, falling to an assassin's bullet.

We need to be passionate and uncompromising for God's truth, like the apostle Paul and our sixteenth president. At times it will be pricey and painful, but it is always right.

BE COMPASSIONATE WITH THE SEEKER

Paul's passion for the truth never superseded his compassion for the seeker. Acts 17:22, 23 records, "Paul then stood up in the meeting of the Areopagus and said: 'Men of Athens! I see that in every way you are very religious. For as I walked around and looked carefully at your objects of worship, I even found an altar with this inscription: TO AN UNKNOWN GOD. Now what you worship as something unknown I am going to proclaim to you.'"

Notice what Paul did in Athens: he took people where they were and led them to where they needed to be. He didn't begin with, "Shame on you, Athenians! You ought to know better than to worship these chunks of stone and carvings of wood. Anybody with two brain cells knocking together knows there is only one God. Get a life!" Because Paul understood the culture, he met them where they were so he could lead them to Jesus. What an intriguing approach! Paul hooked them using their own curiosity as bait—he promised to introduce them to the unknown God. No wonder they listened!

We twenty-first century disciples need to take a lesson from Paul. Our passion for the truth should not override our compassion for the seeker. We must meet people where they are in order to have the opportunity to introduce them to Jesus.

I don't mean we compromise our convictions or morality to level the playing field, but we can't expect the nonbeliever to meet us at our level of faith. If we, like Paul, are desperate for others to find the truth, then we will find a genuine way to make it irresistible.

The account in Acts 17 does not end with the words "and they all lived happily ever after." Rather, it reads like this: "When they heard about the resurrection of the dead, some of them sneered, but others said, 'We want to hear you again on this subject'" (v. 32).

Not everyone that day embraced the truth of the gospel, and not everyone will accept it today. However, no one will believe the truth if we fail to present it in a winsome manner and in terms the culture can understand.

BE FAITHFUL, REGARDLESS OF THE RESPONSE

If we aren't careful, we can overlook a very salient point about following the will of God. Paul's plans were interrupted by a divine vision, and the Holy Spirit prevented the mission team from going north (Acts 16:6-10). With such clear direction from God, one might assume that the rest of the journey was smooth sailing. Not so. As a matter of fact, it was anything *but* a pleasant ride. For instance, see what took place in Acts 16, 17—all *before* Paul went to Athens:

o *In Philippi, when Paul cast out an evil spirit that gave a young woman psychic powers, her owners became furious. She lost her fortune-telling ability, and her owners lost their fortune. Paul and Silas were flogged and thrown into prison for that good deed (16:16-24).*

o *In Thessalonica, the team was pursued by an angry mob and had to leave town in the dark of night (17:1-9).*

o *In Berea, the unruly mob from Thessalonica followed them to the nobler community of Berea, and Paul had to be escorted out of that town and taken to Athens (17:10-15).*

Paul was flogged, imprisoned, falsely accused, hated, and threatened. He fled from city to city, hid in the shadows, and traveled under the cover of darkness. His preaching was ridiculed, rejected, and reviled. And all of this happened because he was following the route assigned by God!

At times we erroneously conclude that if God is leading and we are following, all will be pleasant and profitable. Unfortunately, there is no eleventh commandment or bonus beatitude that offers such assurance. God takes great delight in working through our adversities, infirmities, and anxieties. When we are weak, God is at his best. Be faithful! When you follow him, his plan and purpose will be accomplished. In the midst of Paul's sufferings in Philippi, one of the most positive congregations was born, Lydia gave her life to Christ (Acts 16:15), and the Philippian jailer's family was converted (vv. 33, 34). Who can put a price tag on such eternal victories?

When you choose to leave your backyard, you will find people very similar to the people Paul found in ancient Europe. Today's seekers absolutely need a genuine relationship with you so they can discover a genuine relationship with God.

o   *Be passionate about the truth and compassionate with the seeker.*

o   *Be ready with a plan, but expect interruptions.*

o   *Be faithful, most of all—you may be the only hope a hopeless world ever meets.*

Whether you circumnavigate the globe during your life or you touch the lives of neighbors just beyond your hedge, give them the one truth they cannot live without—give them Jesus.

I discovered this letter in the *Christian Record*, which was published in Indianapolis, Indiana, in 1867. A preacher named William F. Mavity had moved to Indiana to preach, and reported his observations after eighteen months of ministry:

> I have confined my labors to Southern Indiana from motives of benevolence. The churches here are more destitute of efficient proclaimers than any other part of the State.
>
> But, thank God, this dark corner is illuminated by the faithful teaching of B. T. Goodman, Ira and Sylvester Scott, A. and L. Conner, Wood, Mitchell, Lang, McKinney and Miller; a self-sacrificing band, who, in devotion to the cause they have

espoused, would have been an honor to the Grecian heroes who bled and conquered at Marathon. . . . They have no such word as "fail" in their vocabulary, but are worthy to be pleaders of the cause plead by Barton W. Stone . . . and many others, now in Paradise.[7]

Finding that letter was like personally discovering buried treasure, for several reasons. My great-great-grandfather, Abner Conner, was among those mentioned. I discovered a heritage of encouragement. When I read William Mavity's 1867 report, I was also reminded that this band of brothers had established the very congregation where I grew up and met Jesus Christ. If not for their efforts, I might not know the Lord today. They moved beyond the hedge and planted several churches throughout the southern part of the state, and the product of their efforts continues to this day.

Then it struck me: If their efforts are still making a global difference 140 years later, what we do today will still be making a difference long after we are gone. I can only hope and pray that thousands of people in the twenty-*third* century will come to know Christ because of what we are doing right now. The world is waiting for us to get beyond the hedge with God's truth. May there be no such word as *fail* in our vocabulary!

1 You can see them in many of the backyards of American neighborhoods or subdivisions. Tall and sometimes decorative, they are aptly named privacy fences.

Do you have a privacy fence? What was your reason for erecting one? Does the congregation where you serve have any "privacy fences" to protect it from changes? How could you go about tearing down those fences?

2 God has a plan for your life too. You may not have discovered it at this point, but it's there. The timing may not be right yet, your training may not be complete, all the pieces may not quite be in place . . . but God has a plan.

Do you ever feel like you have nothing to contribute to the work of Christ? If so, you need to change your perspective. God can and will use each of us to accomplish his will. What can you do to make yourself available to him?

3 Our best-laid plans may be interrupted by God. When Paul and his team left Antioch, they had every intention of going north; but that plan was interrupted by a divine vision.

How do you react to the interruptions that come into your life? Do you see them as annoyances, or opportunities? Try changing your attitude toward interruptions and begin looking for ways in which God may be working.

4 Truth cannot be diminished by our attempts to veil it. We can ignore it, reject it, dismiss it, argue against it, and try to bury it; but like the Energizer Bunny, truth keeps going and going and . . .

Have you ever suffered because of taking a stand for truth? What happened? How was it worth it? In our attempts to be passionate for

the truth, how can we ensure that we will be compassionate toward the seeker? Have you ever allowed your passion for the truth to supersede your compassion for others? What happened? How can the two be compatible?

5 At times we erroneously conclude that if God is leading and we are following, all will be pleasant and profitable. Unfortunately, there is no eleventh commandment or bonus beatitude that offers such assurance. God takes great delight in working through our adversities, infirmities, and anxieties. When we are weak, God is at his best. Be faithful!

Recall a time when you found being faithful a challenge. Have you ever been discouraged when you were trying to follow faithfully but kept running into roadblocks? Describe the experience. What positive steps can you take to ensure that your faithfulness is not weakened by tough times?

The name of Jesus is the one lever that lifts the world.
ANONYMOUS

Names are the unique and personal monikers by which we are known. Sometimes a particular name really fits a person's character or career. As a teenager I was once referred to a dermatologist named Dr. Slaughter. After an uncomfortable treatment on my face, I understood the connection!

Here are some more interesting names I've run across:

o   *Peter Abbot, a veterinarian*

o   *Chester Drawers, a furniture salesman*

o   *Ross Weed, a professional landscaper*

One of my favorite parts of the Saturday morning PBS radio program *Car Talk* is the credits listing at the conclusion of the show. Obviously, most names are imaginary, but the creativity of those names is delightful. Here are a few you might hear as *Car Talk* slips off the air:

o   *Phillip Airtime, broadcast philosopher*

o   *Dustin Dubree, construction manager*

o   *Cody Pendant, coordinator, 12-step recovery program*

o   *Erin Spelling, proofreader*

o   *Upton Leftus, director of employee loyalty program[1]*

Some names are both creative *and* real! One of the members of our church staff has a sister whose maiden name was Candy Cain. In southern Indiana where I grew up, there was a family whose surname was Christmas. What do you suppose they named their daughter? You guessed it—Mary!

With the passing of time, certain names become synonymous with greatness: Abraham Lincoln, Helen Keller, and George Washington Carver are three such examples. Others will always be synonymous with evil: names like Jezebel, Adolph Hitler, and Saddam Hussein come to mind. At best some are just . . . well, unusual. Consider Arthur Pepper's daughter, nicknamed Alphabet Pepper, or Alpha for short. She acquired her nickname because her father named her Anna Bertha Cecilia Diana Emily Fanny Gertrude Hypatia Inez Jane Kate Louisa Maud Nora Ophelia Quince Rebecca Starkey Teresa Ulysis Venus Winifred Xenophon Yetty Zeus Pepper—one name for every letter in the alphabet, with *P* for Pepper displaced to the end.[2]

Regardless of how unique, unusual, or strange a name may appear, it is special to someone in this world. There is, however, one name that stands above all other names: Jesus Christ. His is the only name that can eternally transform a life from the inside out.

That truth became especially apparent one day in first-century Jerusalem.

DISABLED FROM BIRTH

Before the apostle Paul's conversion to Christ and his subsequent rise to become the central character of early church history, Simon Peter was prominent in many of the early adventures. Acts 3 opens with Peter and

John headed to the temple at the afternoon time of prayer. (In Bible days there were at least two daily times for prayer.) It was an ordinary day—no special holiday or religious festival—just the daily devotional of prayer at 3:00 PM.

The Beautiful Gate, made of expensive bronze, was considered the main entrance and was the largest of the temple gates. Located on the east side of the temple grounds and fifteen steps above the courtyard level, it must have been an especially breathtaking sight in the morning sun. People with disabilities, however—those who were crippled, blind, and maimed—were not allowed to pass through the Beautiful Gate into the court of Israel; the fifteen steps were as close as they could get to the actual temple itself.[3]

Based on the Old Testament commands, the Hebrew culture of that day was known for its charity. The disabled who could not work depended upon the generosity and compassion of those who could. To compensate for their inability to provide for their own personal needs, the disabled had only one recourse: they begged. To make the most of a benevolent situation, one needed visibility in an obvious place. Where better to touch the hearts of people than in front of the main gate to the place of worship? Thus the fifteen steps leading up to the gate called Beautiful were often lined with people begging.

One of those who occupied a few square feet of stone in the shadow of the huge bronze doors had been disabled from birth. Imagine what that was like: He had never experienced the joy of walking in the grass, running down the street, or jumping in the air to catch a lightning bug. He could not move about from place to place without the aid of another human being. Without question, much of his life had been spent on or near those steps. Day in and day out those stones had become his home away from home. What a boring, demoralizing, and humiliating existence!

He begged and pleaded for what was not his; he totally depended on the compassion of others without being able to offer anything in return.

How many people do you think ever made any eye contact with him? Few, if any, I would guess. That shouldn't surprise us. When you pull up to an intersection and someone is standing there holding a cardboard sign that reads Will Work for Food, do you make eye contact, or look straight ahead? Most of us look straight ahead. Once eye contact is made, the will to say no weakens.

While I was on a mission trip to India, I experienced a very common occurrence. It is routine for beggars to step right up to stopped vehicles. They stepped right up to ours too. They pounded on the windows of our van to attract attention and then pleaded their case for money. On the street it got even more personal. They approached and touched us as we walked along.

Broken and pathetic in appearance, these beggars often carried in their arms sick-looking babies that tore at my heart. Despite the obvious need, we were told not to give them money because they didn't get to keep it. They were only the pawns in a much bigger scam. Still, I learned I could not make eye contact if I wanted to say no.

HEALED FOR LIFE

The beggar at the Beautiful Gate didn't have much of a life. He saw hundreds of people daily who probably never really saw him. I'm sure his words sounded mechanical—he'd voiced them thousands of times with only minimal response. As Peter and John approached the huge gateway, this disabled man launched into his spiel: "I've been this way from birth . . . have pity on me, won't you? A shekel or mite will help me eat one more day."

Only a few coins had been sprinkled in the bottom of his beggar's basket; and it was, by that time, mid-afternoon. Just another empty effort in the life of this Jerusalem beggar. But what may have appeared to him as an ordinary day was about to become the most extraordinary day of his dull life. After years of lying in the shadow of the big bronze doors, he was about to step through those doors into the temple courts for the first time ever.

That the man was just going through the motions seems evident from the fact that Peter and John forced him to make eye contact (Acts 3:4). That was something new. Then Peter said, "Silver or gold I do not have, but what I have I give you. In the name of Jesus Christ of Nazareth, walk" (v. 6).

Nothing.

The man obviously felt nothing and made no attempt to move. He may have wondered, *Who are these clowns, and who is this Jesus they are talking about?* Peter, having had years of pulling fishing nets out of the sea, knew what to do. He reached down, grabbed the disabled man's right hand, and pulled him to his feet.

Instantly, the man's legs, ankles, and feet were made whole and strong. He took a small jump. *Will the joints hold?* he must have wondered. Then a bigger jump—no pain. A leap—still no pain. He laughed. He started walking . . . baby steps at first, then full steps, and then a dead run as if he were the post position in a four-man relay. The smile on his face caused his eyes to disappear. The giddy laughter echoed off the bronze doors and drew a crowd. They instantly recognized him as the crippled man; that is, the *former* crippled man. Peter and John watched with a sense of joy, knowing that the healing of the man's feet would not compare to the healing of his soul when he discovered the Jesus behind the name.

The three of them walked up the steps together and through the doors.

The formerly disabled man just couldn't contain himself. Walking seemed too ordinary for such an occasion—every other step was a jump or leap, and the words from his lips were those of heartfelt praise to God. The crowd couldn't believe what they had just witnessed. They gathered around the three of them, and the man-turned-sprinter latched on to the apostles.

Luke is specific in the word he chose in Acts 3:11—the man "held" on to Peter and John with all of his strength. He wasn't about to let these men out of his sight. He owed them and their God his very life.

Crowds tend to attract attention. As more men gathered to check out the commotion (women were not allowed beyond the bronze doors into the court of Israel), the group grew into a gathering, and the gathering mushroomed into a mass of curious seekers. Peter did what any good preacher would do: he preached. And what a sermon it was! That message became a turning point in the life of the first-century church—and all because of the name of Jesus.

As a matter of fact, it was a polarizing sermon. Some welcomed the words about Jesus, while others sought to squelch the name from ever being proclaimed again. Peter and John spent a night in jail for their efforts (Acts 4:3), but it didn't stop them or the church from continuing to serve others in the name of Jesus.

In a question and answer session with about three hundred preachers in India, I was asked if I had ever suffered persecution for my faith. It was the most uncomfortable moment of my journey. I looked around the room at men who faced persecution on a daily basis and was almost embarrassed to admit that I had no scars on my body for Christ. I've never felt more insignificant in my life. Those men stood huge in their faith, and I was lost in their shadows. I marveled at their Christian service in the face of potential beatings, arrest, and even death. If they can serve courageously in the name of Jesus under such adverse circumstances, then surely I can be stronger in my less threatening environment.

You can be stronger too!

PITCH IN AND SERVE

It is called by various names at churches in different parts of the country: a potluck meal, a basket dinner, a linger-longer, a finger-food fellowship, or a pitch-in. Regardless of the name used, the activity is the same—people sharing the food they have prepared with everyone else in the group. I'm convinced that some of the best cooks in the world are in the church! Consequently, a pitch-in is usually a great experience. Usually.

Our family had a very unique experience at a pitch-in dinner. My wife and our daughters had already been through the line when I sat down with my crowded plate of goodies. Just as I was about to dig in, I heard Elsie whisper my name. I could tell by her expression that something was wrong. She nodded at her plate, trying not to attract attention. That's when I noticed more protein on my wife's plate than her taste buds could handle. Smack dab in the middle of the broccoli-rice-and-cheese casserole was a fully cooked cockroach.

From all appearances it had died happy, lying on its back with all legs and antennae intact. As discreetly as possible (so as not to alarm our daughters, who would *not* be discreet at the sight of a roach), I took her plate to the kitchen and buried the evidence in a trash can. Trying to make the moment a little more palatable, I whispered encouragingly, "Look at it this way, dear, finding a whole cockroach is better than finding half of one." She was not amused. And I will admit . . . since that night pitch-ins are less appealing than they used to be.

For the next few pages, let's think of a pitch-in as something other
than refreshment around a table with friends. Think of it in terms of
refreshment through encouraging, supporting, and helping one another in
Jesus' name—a spiritual pitch-in.

PITCH IN AND SERVE IN YOUR DAILY LIFE

God works in extraordinary ways while we are living out our ordinary
lives for him. I've learned that God seldom works through messages
written in the clouds or sends his blessings via some cataclysmic
experience. Occasionally I've seen God intervene in uniquely miraculous
ways to spare a life, restore a marriage, or provide a new job. But mostly
God seems to take great delight in working providentially through the
ordinary courses of life. If you sit back and wait for the skies to open up
and broadcast the audible voice of God before you pitch in, you may
never accomplish anything.

I've never heard the physical voice of God. Many times I have sensed his
leading, but there have also been periods when I have suffered through his
silence. At times I have been confident in his will for my life, but there
have also been times when I agonized over what God wanted *from* me or
for me. During thirty years in ministry, I have learned that God works
best in the interruptions of our daily lives—just as when Peter and John
were interrupted on their way to pray.

Generally we don't like interruptions. You sit down to eat supper and the
doorbell rings; it's a pollster with a political, environmental, or sociological
survey (and yes, a donation appeal along with it). I hurt for the people who
have those jobs, because most of us detest such interruptions:

o   *A car pulls out in front of us and interrupts our cruising speed.*

o   *A baby's birth interrupts our freedom.*

o *An illness interrupts our retirement.*

o *A lost job interrupts our career.*

o *An alarm clock interrupts the best sleep of the night.*

Ricky Kees owned and managed an apartment building in Memphis, Tennessee. He was so disturbed by an alarm clock of one of his tenants that he shot the clock with a .22-caliber revolver—twice—before it would quit buzzing. That move cost him time in jail,[4] which in itself was a major interruption. We don't like interruptions.

But before you dismiss all interruptions as mere annoyances, remember that God may be very much at work in the disruptions of our lives. A dear friend and missionary in Korea had traveled to the States in the summer of 1983 to bring an orphaned infant who was being adopted by an American family. He was scheduled to return on August 31, but numerous interruptions on that day prevented him from arriving at the airport in time to catch his flight. Anxious to return home, he was deeply disheartened at missing his connection. But that disappointment soon turned to gratitude. The flight he missed was Korean Airlines KAL 007 that strayed into Soviet airspace and was tragically shot down over the ocean by Russian jet interceptors.

See! Not all interruptions are negative. As a matter of fact, when we get to Heaven, if God were to allow us to see our lives replayed from his vantage point, we might be amazed at the number of times when interruptions changed—or even saved!—our lives while in this world.

The account in Acts 3 offers another, but less obvious, perspective on interruptions. What for most would have been an annoying interruption to important prayer time became the opportunity to change lives. And not just the life of the disabled man; there were dozens of onlookers that day. Verse 10 says, "They were filled with wonder and amazement." Verses 11-19 show us that the people closed in on Peter and John and listened to them speak. Those people often get overlooked in this story, but their lives were spiritually changed that day because of what they had seen and then heard.

Stop expecting God to move Heaven and earth to get you to do his work. Make the most of every day, taking special note of the interruptions. Often God is providing for you not an interruption, but an opportunity to do something in Jesus' name! Heaven might indeed be moving at that point to change someone's life through you.

In 1937 Walt Disney produced his first full-length animated feature, *Snow White*. When the project began in 1934, it was known derisively as Disney's Folly, but it became a huge success when it was released three years later. Today it remains a classic. Most people have no clue how much went on behind the scenes to create this eighty-four-minute masterpiece. *Snow White* required the "collaboration of nearly six hundred employees who drew, inked, and painted the quarter-million drawings in what totaled two hundred years' worth of man-hours."[5] Each hand-painted cel, or picture, was on the screen for only 1/24 of a second. The end result was incredible, but behind the scenes it was at times a nightmare.

I would suggest that in our own lives we have no comprehension of what is going on behind the scenes. But God does, and he will work out the details to create a masterpiece. Pitch in as you go about your daily life. You might just make history.

PITCH IN AND SERVE AS THE NEED ARISES

The real heart of this Acts 3 event is about meeting a need. The disabled man asked for money just as he had been doing for years, but money could only buy him some food or clothing. The money was merely a bandage on a wound that would not heal. What he really needed he couldn't imagine asking for. What possible response could he have expected from two ordinary Galilean fishermen had he requested: "Sirs, would you heal my feet and ankles?" I don't suppose many of us would have asked either.

It is here that God's awesome nature explodes in the story. The man asked for something temporary, but God gave him that which is eternal and lasting. Giving him new feet wasn't nearly as important as giving him a new heart. The physical healing in the story is the least important result.

Here's the good news: God does the same for us! If God restores your health, it is only a temporary blessing even if you live to be one hundred years old. What the disabled man needed more than anything was Jesus—nothing more, nothing less. That's what all people need. The power in this story isn't about physical healing.

"Yes," you say, "but he was healed physically too." True, but do you think he was the only individual waiting outside the gate that day who was lame, crippled, blind, deaf, or disfigured? No way! It was a place where many came to beg because they could do nothing else. What about *them?* Why didn't the apostles heal every hurting person at the Beautiful Gate? The answer lies in this truth: The purpose of God wasn't in helping one man find the ability to walk; it was in helping the masses find Jesus.

God's purpose hasn't changed in two thousand years. He still wants the masses to find his Son. And that's why we pitch in to serve. It's not about just doing something nice that lasts for a few hours, a few days, or even a few years. We aren't compelled to give what others *want*, but we are compelled to help meet their needs—the greatest of which is finding life in the name of Jesus. Be for others what they *need* you to be, not necessarily what they *want* you to be. Doing anything less could end up being as disheartening for them as . . . well, as finding a cockroach in their casserole!

Sometimes in order to meet a need, you'll be required to step forward at a moment's notice. Thirteen-year-old Natalie Gilbert won the contest. She was going to sing the national anthem before game three of the 2003 NBA play-offs between the Portland Trail Blazers and the Dallas Mavericks. Natalie had practiced flawlessly leading up to that night, but she had spent the day of the game in bed with the flu. Nevertheless, she was determined to sing. She began well; but in the crowded Rose Garden arena, she panicked and forgot the words. In that awkward moment of memory loss, Trail Blazers Coach Maurice Cheeks stepped over and helped her get started again. Coach Mo may know basketball, but he is no singer. Yet his encouraging words and less-than-melodic voice saved the day. Natalie found her place and her voice again. She finished strong, and the crowd applauded in approval.

That situation certainly wasn't what Natalie wanted, but Coach Mo certainly was what she needed. "He totally saved me, I couldn't even remember the words. I tried to start over again, but the words wouldn't come," said Gilbert. "I was walking off afterward and he said to me, 'Don't worry kid, everyone has a bad game once in a while.'"[6]

PITCH IN AND SERVE, ALWAYS GIVING HONOR TO GOD

Not only did the formerly disabled man praise God, so did Peter and John. Neither accepted any credit for the miracle; they simply pointed the witnesses to the power of God at work. More than once the apostles reminded the crowd that the man could now walk because the miracle had been done in the name of Jesus—by his authority, power, and mercy.

An earthly miracle always finds its greatest relevance in a heavenly purpose. God could have led the Israelites to the promised land without a detour through the Red Sea, but that miraculous intervention demonstrated God's greatness in a way that would not be forgotten. God was praised and credited with that act of salvation. Even the pagan nations continued to talk about it for years.

The church universal must serve with one very important purpose in mind. To feed the hungry, care for the suffering, reach out to the homeless, and provide for the poor is to fulfill a biblical mandate. What's more, this ministry of benevolence should be performed with no strings attached. However, if these acts of divine service are an end instead of a means, then we have lost sight of the intention behind Jesus' command. Had Peter and John been interested only in the man's physical condition, the story would have a much different ending—no sermon, no confrontation, no night in prison, and no official rebuke. Most assuredly the name of Jesus would have been a non-issue.

Peter and John looked beyond gnarled ankles and atrophied muscles and saw the opportunity to glorify God and proclaim the name of Jesus. It is a wonderful gesture of kindness when Christians sacrifice time and energy to serve others around them; but if the motive isn't Christ-centered and Heaven-oriented, then the church is no different from any other benevolent civic organization. Peter and John offered much more than a podiatric intervention—they offered life in the name of Jesus! When you serve, does Jesus get the credit? Do you use opportunity for service as a time to introduce people to him?

PITCH IN AND SERVE, REGARDLESS OF THE COST

What did this miracle cost? No silver or gold was expended, but it was costly. The healing stirred up trouble, and it cost Peter and John time in prison.

Most preaching ministers have preached some sleepers—and I've had my fair share throughout the years. But I've never spent a night in jail for what I preached. The Sadducees, who rejected the premise of a resurrection, were incensed by what Peter and John proclaimed as true. Following a night behind bars, Peter and John were hauled in before the Sanhedrin and commanded never to preach in Jesus' name again. That warning had about as much effect as telling a hungry kid not to touch a plate of oven-fresh chocolate chip cookies! They were emboldened in their preaching. Their courage inspired the whole church, and no cost was too great to proclaim the name of Jesus. Serving God is not always easy, or pleasant, but it is always right—regardless of the cost.

In Ronald Reagan's first inaugural address, he referenced the simple white grave markers in Arlington Memorial Cemetery:

> Under one such marker lies a young man, Martin Treptow, who left his job in a small town barber shop in 1917 to go to France with the famed Rainbow Division. There, on the western front, he was killed trying to carry a message between battalions under heavy artillery fire.

> We're told that on his body was found a diary. On the flyleaf under the heading "My Pledge," he had written these words: "America must win this war. Therefore I will work, I will save, I will sacrifice, I will endure, I will fight cheerfully and do my utmost, as if the issue of the whole struggle depended on me alone."[7]

Some might conclude that Martin Treptow was just a foot soldier. He *knew* better. His purpose was to willingly give all in the name of his country. Not a bad model for those of us in the kingdom of God. God has called us to willingly give all as we serve in the name of Jesus. How about it? Pitch in and make a difference for the sake and honor of Christ. Just imagine what God has in mind for you beyond your backyard!

1 Regardless of how unique, unusual, or strange a name may appear, it is special to someone in this world. There is, however, one name that stands above all other names: Jesus Christ. His is the only name that can eternally transform a life from the inside out.

Do you like your name, or would you prefer a different one? How important is it that people know your name? How important is it that people know about the name of Jesus from you? What are you doing to make sure that happens?

2 Generally we don't like interruptions. . . . A baby's birth interrupts our freedom. An illness interrupts our retirement. A lost job interrupts our career. An alarm clock interrupts the best sleep of the night. . . . Before you dismiss all interruptions as mere annoyances, remember that God may be very much at work in the disruptions.

Do you suppose Peter and John first thought of the disabled man as an interruption to a very important commitment? How often do you dismiss an interruption as an annoyance before you look for the opportunity? What can you do to retrain your mind to think differently about such interruptions?

3 The real heart of this Acts 3 account is about meeting a need. The disabled man asked for money just as he had been doing for years, but money could only buy him some food or clothing. The money was merely a bandage on a wound that would not heal. What he really needed he couldn't imagine asking for.

Who among us would have asked for a miracle from a couple of fishermen? How do we distinguish between meeting a want and meeting a need? What can you do to help people look past their physical circumstances and see the more important spiritual needs in their lives?

4 An earthly miracle always finds its greatest relevance in a heavenly purpose. . . . It is a wonderful gesture of kindness when Christians sacrifice time and energy to serve others around them; but if the motive isn't Christ-centered and Heaven-oriented, then the church is no different from any other benevolent civic organization.

There is a fine line between a random act of kindness and being benevolent in the name of Jesus. Even though it's not wrong to just be kind, why is it important to distinguish between the two? How can you be kind and compassionate with no strings attached and still fulfill the purpose of God by introducing people to Jesus?

INTRODUCTION

1. Learn more about this ministry at http://www.sportsoutreach.com.

CHAPTER 1

1. Material in this section was taken from http://www.oberlin.edu/external/EOG/OYTT-images/ ElishaGray.html (accessed July 17, 2007).

2. Bill Adler Jr. and Julie Houghton, *America's Stupidest Business Decisions: 101 Blunders, Flops, and Screwups* (New York: William Morrow and Company, 1997), 94.

3. Ibid., 119.

4. Ibid., 171.

5. http://www.allheadlinenews.com/articles/7000144 784 (accessed July 27, 2007).

6. Jim Collins, *Good to Great: Why Some Companies Make the Leap . . . and Others Don't* (New York: HarperCollins, 2001), 12–13.

7. Edward K. Rowell, *Quotes and Idea Starters for Preaching and Teaching* (Grand Rapids, MI: Baker, 1996), 121.

CHAPTER 2

1. Material in this section was taken from http://www.castletown.com/Brothers.htm (accessed July 27, 2007) and http://www.homeofheroes.com/brotherhood/sullivans2.html (accessed August 10, 2007).

2. http://www.salary.com/aboutus/layoutscripts/abtl_default.asp?tab=abt&cat=cat012&ser=ser041& part=Par640&isdefault=0 (accessed July 27, 2007) and www.cnn.com/2007/US/05/02/mothers. worth/index.html (accessed July 27, 2007).

3. U.S. Census Bureau, "Geographical Mobility: 2002 to 2003," http://www.census.gov/prod/ 2004pubs/p20-549.pdf (accessed June 5, 2007).

4. "Marriage Mayhem," *Campus Life*, March 1981, 31.

5. Peggy L. Barta, "Blended Families: How to Make Sense of Your New Stepfamily," *In Touch* APS Healthcare newsletter, vol. 1, issue 2, http://www.washington.edu/admin/hr/benefits/worklife/ carelink/intouch/intouch_blnded_fam.pdf (accessed May 31, 2007).

6. The summary of the episode can be found at: http://www.littlehouseonprairie.com/season1/ episode-6-if-i-should-wake-before-i-die.html (accessed July 27, 2007).

CHAPTER 3

1. Deborah Deford, ed., *Quotable Quotes* (Pleasantville, NY: Reader's Digest, 1997), 42.

2. Edward K. Rowell, *Quotes and Idea Starters for Preaching and Teaching* (Grand Rapids, MI: Baker, 1996), 51.

CHAPTER 4

1. Mark C. Black, *The College Press NIV Commentary: Luke* (Joplin, MO: College Press Publishing Company, 1996), 201–202.

2. John Winthrop, sermon "A Model of Christian Charity," the Winthrop Society, http://www. winthropsociety.org/doc_charity.php (accessed July 27, 2007).

3. Robert C. Shannon, *1,000 Windows: A Speaker's Sourcebook of Illustrations* (Cincinnati: Standard Publishing, 1997), 211.

CHAPTER 5

1. Material in this section was taken from http://www.scvhistory.com/scvhistory/signal/ newsmaker/sg020104.htm (accessed July 27, 2007).

2. Craig S. Keener, ed., *The IVP Bible Background Commentary: New Testament* (Downers Grove, IL: InterVarsity Press, 1993), 240.

3. http://www.sermoncentral.com (accessed July 27, 2007).

CHAPTER 6

1. Mark C. Black, *The College Press NIV Commentary: Luke* (Joplin, MO: College Press Publishing Company, 1996), 358–359.

2. Mark E. Moore, *The Chronological Life of Christ, Volume 2: From Galilee to Glory* (Joplin, MO: College Press Publishing Company, 1997), 265.

3. Herbert Lockyer, *All the Men of the Bible* (Grand Rapids, MI: Zondervan Publishing House, 1958), 226.

4. Dale Carnegie, *How to Win Friends and Influence People* (New York: Simon & Schuster, Inc., 1936, revised 1981), 4.

5. Ibid., 105.

6. Ronald Reagan in an informal exchange with reporters, http://www.presidency.ucsb.edu/ws/ index.php?pid=36103 (accessed July 27, 2007).

CHAPTER 7

1. Thomas L. Friedman, *The World Is Flat: A Brief History of the Twenty-first Century* (New York: Farrar, Straus and Giroux, 2005), 40–41.

2. A. Rupprecht, "Athens," *The Zondervan Pictorial Encyclopedia of the Bible*, vol. 1, ed. Merrill C. Tenney (Grand Rapids, MI: Zondervan Publishing House, 1975, 1976), 403–406.

3. E. M. Blaiklock, "Tarsus," *The Zondervan Pictorial Encyclopedia of the Bible*, vol. 5, ed. Merrill C. Tenney (Grand Rapids, MI: Zondervan Publishing House, 1975, 1976), 598–603.

4. Deborah Deford, ed., *Quotable Quotes* (Pleasantville, NY: Reader's Digest, 1997), 158.

5. *Quotations of Abraham Lincoln* (Bedford, MA: Applewood Books, 2003), 22.

6. Ibid., 26.

7. James M. Mathes, ed., *The Christian Record*, vol. 1, no. 3, March 1867, 91.

CHAPTER 8

1. http://www.cartalk.com/content/about/credits/credits.html (accessed July 31, 2007).

2. http://anglo-celtic-connections.blogspot.com/2007/06/unusual-names.html (accessed July 31, 2007).

3. Craig S. Keener, ed., *The IVP Bible Background Commentary: New Testament* (Downers Grove, IL: InterVarsity Press, 1993), 330–331.

4. "Strange But True," http://taylor.250x.com/StrangeBut/StrangeButTrue56.html (accessed July 31, 2007).

5. Neal Gabler, *Walt Disney: The Triumph of the American Imagination* (New York: Alfred A. Knopf, 2006), 273.

6. "Cheeks Anthem Assist," http://www.nba.com/blazers/features/Cheeks_Anthem_Assist-73713-41.html (accessed July 31, 2007).

7. Ronald Reagan's first inaugural address, January 20, 1981, Ronald Reagan Presidential Foundation and Library, http://www.reaganfoundation.org/reagan/speeches/first.asp (accessed July 31, 2007).

To learn more about the author
please visit
www.tdellsworth.com

Also available . . .

- Second Guessing God
  978-0-7847-1841-4

- Second Guessing God (discussion guide)
  0-7847-1958-6

- Free Refill
  978-0-7847-1912-1

- Free Refill (discussion guide)
  978-0-7847-1992-3

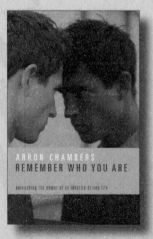

- Remember Who You Are
  978-0-7847-2065-3

Order these titles at
www.standardpub.com
or call 1-800-543-1353

- Soul Craving
  978-0-7847-1955-8

- Soul Craving (discussion guide)
  978-0-7847-1993-0